HUMAN RIGHTS

IN NORTHERN IRELAND

A Helsinki Watch Report

Human Rights Watch

New York • Washington • Los Angeles • London

TABLE OF CONTENTS

FREQUENTLY USED ABBREVIATIONS

ACE	Action for Community Employment
AI	Amnesty International
BBC	British Broadcasting Corporation
CAJ	Committee on the Administration of Justice (The Northern Ireland Civil Liberties Council)
CSCE	Conference on Security and Cooperation in Europe
DCC	Deputy Chief Constable
DED	Department of Economic Development
DPP	Director of Public Prosecution
ECHR	European Convention on Human Rights
EPA	NI (Emergency Provisions) Act of 1991
IBA	Independent Broadcasting Authority
ICPC	Independent Commission on Police Complaints
ICCPR	International Covenant on Civil and Political Rights
ICRC	International Committee of the Red Cross
INLA	Irish National Liberation Army
IPLO	Irish People's Liberation Organization
IRA	Irish Republican Army
NCCL	National Council for Civil Liberties (Liberty)
NIO	Northern Ireland Office
PACE	Police and Criminal Evidence (NI) Order 1989
PTA	Prevention of Terrorism (Temporary Provisions) Act of 1989
RUC	Royal Ulster Constabulary
SACHR	Standing Advisory Commission on Human Rights
SDLP	Social Democratic and Labor Party
SPA	Civil Authorities (Special Powers) Act (NI) 1922
UDR	Ulster Defense Regiment
UVF	Ulster Volunteer Force
UFF	Ulster Freedom Fighters
UDA	Ulster Defense Association

ACKNOWLEDGMENTS

This report is based largely on information gathered by Norman Dorsen, Stokes Professor of Law at New York University Law School and former president of the American Civil Liberties Union, David Rudovsky, Senior Fellow at the University of Pennsylvania Law School and a lawyer in private practice, and Lois Whitman, Deputy Director of Helsinki Watch, during a Helsinki Watch fact-finding mission to Northern Ireland from January 2 to 12, 1991. The report was written by the members of the mission.

Before and during our trip to Northern Ireland, the British Information Service and the Northern Ireland Office were extremely helpful in arranging appointments with government and security officials with whom we asked to meet and in providing us with requested documents. We appreciate their cooperation and their willingness to accommodate our tight schedule. We also appreciate the time and helpfulness of officials in the Republic of Ireland and in Great Britain whom we visited in Dublin and London.

Without the exhaustive efforts in Belfast of the Committee on the Administration of Justice, particularly of Martin O'Brien and Michael Ritchie, our trip might not have been possible. Their efficiency in arranging interviews with non-government individuals and groups and in providing us with information and assistance made it possible for us to talk with scores of citizens of Northern Ireland of all walks of life and points of view. We are deeply grateful.

Norman Dorsen
David Rudovsky
Lois Whitman

October 1991

I. INTRODUCTION

A state of emergency has existed in Northern Ireland since its partition from the Irish Free State in 1922. Various emergency laws enacted during this seventy-year period have given security forces--the police and the British Army--broad powers to stop people on the street, to question and search them, to search their homes, to detain them for as long as seven days without charges, and to exclude people from Northern Ireland or Great Britain. Even the right to trial by jury has been suspended. Political violence is a daily occurrence, and death is commonplace;   about 2,900 people have died in political violence associated with "The Troubles" since 1969.

At the time of partition, following an uprising and extensive disturbances, the six northeast counties of Ireland were separated from the other 26 counties and became the United Kingdom province of Northern Ireland. The 26 counties became the Irish Free State and subsequently, in 1949, the Republic of Ireland, independent from the United Kingdom.

The population of Northern Ireland is about 1.5 million, of whom about 60 percent are Protestant and 40 percent Catholic. Protestants are largely Unionists--people who want to maintain the union with the United Kingdom. Most Catholics, on the other hand, are Nationalists, who wish to reunite with the Republic of Ireland, which has a population of about 3.5 million, of whom 95 percent are Catholic.[1]

For fifty years Northern Ireland governed itself through a Parliament at Stormont Castle in Belfast. The province was relatively stable from the mid-1920's until the mid-1960's. But following a resurgence of politically-motivated violence in the late 1960's, the United Kingdom prorogued -- or discontinued -- the Stormont Parliament in 1972 and instituted direct rule of Northern Ireland from the UK Parliament in Westminster.

---

[1] Some Unionists call themselves "Loyalists," some of whom support the use of violence for political ends. Some Nationalists call themselves "Republicans," some of whom support the use of violence for political ends.

It is widely acknowledged that during the Stormont period Catholics suffered serious discrimination in employment, housing and political representation. This discrimination led, in the mid- and late 1960's, to peaceful civil rights demonstrations which were met by Unionist resistance, including violence by some Unionists and, on occasion, by the Royal Ulster Constabulary (RUC), the Northern Ireland police. This, in turn, led to the re-emergence of the Irish Republican Army (IRA), a Nationalist paramilitary group, and of comparable Unionist paramilitary groups (chiefly the Ulster Volunteer Force (UVF)).

British troops were sent to Northern Ireland in 1969 and quieted things for a brief period, but violence soon erupted again. In 1972, at the peak of the violence, there were 467 deaths, 1800 explosions and over 10,000 shooting incidents. In 1990, there were 76 deaths, 287 explosions and 396 shooting incidents.[2]

Of the death toll through 1989, 54 percent were civilians with no known connection to paramilitary groups, 31 percent were police or army, and 13 percent were paramilitaries.[3] Of more than 32,000 people injured, about two-thirds were civilians.[4]

Emergency legislation to deal with political violence began with the Civil Authorities (Special Powers) Act (NI). In effect from 1922 until 1973, this act provided police with broad powers to search and arrest, to

---

[2] The murder rate is, however, lower than that in the United States and in many other countries, including Canada, Australia and West Germany. According to the Northern Ireland Office, in 1986 Northern Ireland had a murder rate of 6 per 100,000. This compared with rates of 22 per 100,000 in New York City, 31 in Washington, D.C., and 59 in Detroit. *The Day of Men and Women of Peace Must Surely Come*, Northern Ireland Office, July 1989, p. 36.

[3] See Table I in Chapter III, taken from the Irish Information Partnership, a non-governmental group that until recently published statistical information on Northern Ireland.

[4] *The Day of Men and Women of Peace Must Surely Come*, Northern Ireland Office, July 1989, p. 36.

intern suspects without trial, to seize property, and to ban publications and demonstrations.

Since repeal of the Special Powers Act, police powers to deal with political violence have been provided by the Northern Ireland (Emergency Provisions) Act (EPA), originally enacted in 1973, and the Prevention of Terrorism (Temporary Provisions) Act (the PTA), in effect since 1974. The EPA applies only to Northern Ireland; the PTA applies to all of the United Kingdom. Both acts have been regularly renewed by the UK Parliament.

These emergency acts provide the authorities with extensive powers to deal with the unrest in Northern Ireland, including:

> * the power to stop and search people--anyone can be required to answer questions regarding his or her identity and recent movements;
>
> * the power to arrest, detain and interrogate suspects for up to seven days without a criminal charge and without an appearance before a judge;
>
> * the power to search residences without prior judicial authorization;
>
> * the power to exclude people from Northern Ireland, England or all of the United Kingdom without a trial and without judicial review; and
>
> * the power to detain people by executive order (this power of "internment" has not been used since 1976).
>
> The legislation also:
>
> * declares certain paramilitary organizations illegal and makes membership in them a criminal offense;
>
> * suspends trial by jury for a large number of "scheduled offenses," including murder, armed robbery, possession of explosives, and certain lesser offenses; and

3

* sets a lower standard for the admissibility of confessions than is applicable in the rest of the UK.

The UK has enacted other legislation and issued administrative orders that affect people charged with or suspected of connections with politically-motivated violence:

* the 1988 Criminal Evidence (Northern Ireland) Order curtails the right of suspects not to have inferences drawn from their silence; and

* the Broadcasting Ban ordered by the Home Secretary in 1988 forbids direct radio or television interviews with members of paramilitary groups and certain other organizations, including Sinn Fein, a lawful organization that acts as the political arm of the IRA.

*   *   *

Helsinki Watch was asked to send a fact-finding mission to Northern Ireland by people who believed that a report by an impartial group might provide a helpful appraisal of human rights abuses in the province and bring public attention to conditions there. For that reason, in January 1991 Helsinki Watch sent three people to Northern Ireland in its first mission to the United Kingdom.[5] Over a ten-day period, the Helsinki Watch mission met with human rights activists, lawyers, community workers, religious and political leaders, and government and security officials. The mission interviewed scores of people from both the Catholic and Protestant communities who alleged that they or members of their families had been victims of abuses by security forces or

---

[5] The three members of the fact-finding mission were Norman Dorsen, Stokes Professor of Law at the New York University School of Law, and president of the American Civil Liberties Union from 1976 to 1991, David Rudovsky, Senior Fellow at the University of Pennsylvania Law School and a lawyer in private practice, and Lois Whitman, a lawyer and Deputy Director of Helsinki Watch.

4

paramilitary groups.[6] Most of the interviews took place in Belfast, but some were with people in London/Derry,[7] Omagh, Armagh, Lurgan and Newry. The mission met with government officials and representatives of political parties and other non-government groups in Dublin and in London as well as in Belfast.

The Helsinki Watch mission concluded that human rights abuses are persistent and on-going, that they affect Protestants and Catholics alike, and that they are committed by both security forces and paramilitary groups in violation of international human rights and humanitarian laws and standards. It was saddening to find such extensive human rights violations in a democracy like the United Kingdom, and puzzling as to why they had persisted for so long. Recommendations are set forth in detail in Chapter X.

As to some of the specific findings of the mission: over half (54.4 percent) of the 2,900 deaths since 1969 have been of civilians with no known connection to political violence. Another 31.1 percent have been police or soldiers. Paramilitary groups make up the rest; 10.6 percent of the deaths were of Republican paramilitaries (Nationalists who favor a unified Ireland) and 2.6 percent were Loyalists (Unionists who favor maintaining union with the United Kingdom).

The mission found the level of violence by paramilitary groups appalling: paramilitaries accounted for 2,313 deaths between 1969 and 1989--1,608 people were killed by Republicans and 705 by Loyalists. And most of those killed, 1,206, were civilians with no known connection to political violence (574 of these were killed by Republicans and 632 by Loyalists). During the same period, Republican paramilitaries killed 847 members of security forces, and Loyalist paramilitaries 10.

---

[6] In most cases, the Helsinki Watch mission was not in a position to verify these allegations. Where allegations have been substantiated by court decisions, we have indicated as much.

[7] Unionists call that city Londonderry; Nationalists call it Derry. In this report, we refer to the city as London/Derry.

Paramilitary groups use such barbaric tactics as the Irish Republican Army's "human bombs"--people strapped into vehicles loaded with explosives and sent to bomb security checkpoints--as well as bombs aimed at civilian targets. Loyalists carry out "tit-for-tat" killings by going into Catholic areas and killing Catholics at random in revenge for Republican killings of Loyalists. The level of violence presents serious problems for law enforcement officials.

Helsinki Watch believes that killings of civilians by paramilitary groups violate international humanitarian law. In addition, killings by paramilitary groups of security force members and opposing paramilitaries violate the principles underlying customary international humanitarian law. Helsinki Watch urges paramilitary organizations in both communities to put an end to such violence.

As for killings carried out by security forces, the Helsinki Watch mission found that police and soldiers killed 329 people between 1969 and 1989; of these, 178 were civilians, 123 were Republican paramilitaries, 13 were Loyalist paramilitaries, and 15 were themselves security force members. Helsinki Watch believes that the United Kingdom should enact legislation that strictly controls the use of lethal force in Northern Ireland. The legal standard for the use of deadly force by security forces at present is "such force as is reasonable in the circumstances." The mission found that the reasonableness standard provides too much leeway for the use of lethal force and leads inevitably to abuses. Helsinki Watch recommends that the standard be "absolute necessity"--that is, deadly force should be permitted only when *absolutely necessary*, and only *in proportion* to the actual danger encountered by security forces.

The use of plastic bullets--supposedly non-lethal weapons--for crowd control has also resulted in fatal shootings. Fourteen people have been killed by plastic bullets fired by security forces since 1973. Helsinki Watch recommends that the government ban the use of the plastic bullet.

The Helsinki Watch mission found that security force members who have killed civilians or paramilitaries are rarely prosecuted. Since 1969, police or soldiers have been prosecuted in only nineteen cases in which killings took place while they were on duty. And in only three of these cases have defendants been found guilty of murder or

6

manslaughter. The only member of the regular British Army to have been found guilty of a murder committed while on duty received a life sentence, but he was released after serving only two years and three months of his sentence, and was allowed to rejoin his regiment.

Helsinki Watch recommends thorough, prompt and impartial investigations of all cases in which lethal force is used by security forces. Further, it urges that officers who abuse their investigative powers be appropriately disciplined. The failure to discipline officers properly in the past has led to a high level of public cynicism concerning the accountability of security officers. Additional recommendations are spelled out in the body of this report.

One problem in prosecuting security forces is that, once a police officer or soldier intentionally kills someone, he or she may be charged only with the offense of murder; no lesser charge, such as manslaughter, can be filed. The Helsinki Watch mission found that this requirement is a major barrier to prosecuting security forces. Helsinki Watch recommends that the lesser charges of manslaughter and unreasonable or excessive use of force be added to the Northern Ireland Criminal Code for cases involving the use of lethal force by security forces.

Because police or soldiers are so rarely prosecuted for fatal shootings, often the only time a family can discover what happened to the person who was shot and killed is during a coroner's inquest. The Helsinki Watch mission found that coroners' inquests are subject to inordinate delays, that coroners' juries are not permitted to reach full verdicts, that security force members implicated in deaths are not required to testify, and that victims' families and their attorneys are denied access to evidence before the inquests begin. Helsinki Watch recommends that the Coroners' Laws and Rules in Northern Ireland be brought into line with the laws and rules in England and Wales.

The Helsinki Watch mission found significant problems in detention, including long periods of detention, physical abuse of detainees, and delays in permitting access to counsel. The UK's Prevention of Terrorism Act permits detentions for up to seven days. The European Convention on Human Rights requires that detainees be brought "promptly" before a judge. In 1988, the European Court of Human Rights ruled that a detention of four days and six hours did not meet the "promptness" requirement. The UK then formally derogated from that provision of the European Convention. Helsinki Watch recommends that the UK repeal its derogation and assure that detainees are brought before a court within 48 hours.

The Helsinki Watch mission heard many charges of physical abuse of suspects in detention from both detainees and attorneys. Some of these charges have been sustained by court decisions. Helsinki Watch recommends that the Royal Ulster Constabulary (RUC) investigate all such charges, appropriately discipline the officers responsible, and institute procedures to halt such practices. Helsinki Watch also recommends the video- and audiotaping of all interrogations with strict regulations against unwarranted disclosure.

The mission also found that a detainee's access to his or her attorney is frequently delayed; Helsinki Watch recommends that detainees have immediate and regular access to attorneys.

The power to intern without trial remains part of the emergency laws of Northern Ireland, although it has not been used for fifteen years. Helsinki Watch recommends that such power be abolished.

The Helsinki Watch mission found that security forces frequently stop, search and question people on the street, and concluded that such treatment is sometimes inhuman and degrading. In addition, police and army have conducted thousands of destructive house searches, some of which appear to violate Northern Ireland laws, and a high percentage of which do not produce weapons or equipment used for bombings. Helsinki Watch recommends that search and entry powers be made contingent upon a judicial warrant, absent exigent circumstances.

The Helsinki Watch mission found that the right to a fair trial has been significantly compromised. First, the right to trial by jury has been withdrawn from defendants in cases that allegedly involve political violence ("scheduled offenses"). Helsinki Watch recommends the gradual resumption of jury trials for scheduled offenses, with full protection accorded to witnesses and jurors, and a provision giving a defendant the right to waive a jury trial. Helsinki Watch also concludes that the list of scheduled offenses is over-inclusive, and recommends that the number of scheduled offenses be reduced. The Attorney General should be required to "schedule in" those cases s/he believes should be tried in the non-jury Diplock courts, rather than to include automatically all scheduled offense cases, "scheduling out" only a few.

The Helsinki Watch mission found that the standard for the admissibility of confessions in Diplock Courts permits the admission into evidence of unreliable confessions, some of which may have been secured by abusive treatment in detention. Helsinki Watch recommends that the Emergency Provisions Act standard for the admissibility of confessions be abolished and that the standards used for ordinary offenses be used for scheduled offenses as well.

The Helsinki Watch mission found that the right to silence has been eroded by new rules that permit a court to take adverse inferences from a person's refusal to speak to police during the investigatory stage of a case or to testify in court. Helsinki Watch recommends that the Criminal Evidence (NI) Order 1988 be amended to remove the provision that allows such adverse inferences to be taken.

The Prevention of Terrorism Act provides for orders excluding from Northern Ireland or Great Britain people suspected of involvement with terrorism. These people have been excluded without a hearing and without notice of the charges against them--a form of internal exile. Those who are excluded are simply informed that they are suspected of involvement with terrorism. Helsinki Watch recommends that the PTA orders of exclusion be abolished.

The mission also found that the right to free expression has been significantly cut back--a Broadcasting Ban forbids a person to speak his or her own words on radio or television, and many documentaries, films and interviews have been censored or banned entirely. Helsinki Watch recommends the rescission of the Broadcasting Ban.

A complete list of recommendations is contained in Chapter X.

*   *   *

The turbulent history of Northern Ireland, with its contemporary echoes, provides a backdrop to the human rights situation in the region that cannot be ignored. But this report deals only with the current state

9

of human rights in Northern Ireland, and not with politics or political solutions.

II. ARREST, SEARCH, DETENTION
AND INTERROGATION

Since 1972, when the British government imposed direct rule on Northern Ireland, all laws pertaining to security and police and Army powers in Northern Ireland have been imposed by the UK Parliament. The two most important statutes concerning security and justice are the Northern Ireland (Emergency Provisions) Act of 1991 (EPA) and the Prevention of Terrorism (Temporary Provisions) Act of 1989 (PTA). These statutes supplanted the earlier Special Powers Act and establish a system of security and criminal justice that in many respects is sharply different from the measures in effect in the rest of the United Kingdom.[8]

Although there is a clear dichotomy between the procedures that have been adopted for the investigation and prosecution of "normal" criminal activity and "terrorist" crime, in practice there is significant overlap. Police powers and procedures that were intended to apply only to terrorist activity have reportedly become a common mode of law enforcement and judicial operations.

---

[8] Since direct rule was instituted, government commissions have reviewed the security and criminal justice systems. Lord Diplock, reporting for the first commission in 1972, recommended that internment by the military, as the means for controlling terrorism, be replaced by a security system relying on the police and courts. The Diplock Commission also recommended discontinuance of jury trials for terrorist offenses, a measure that was adopted and continues in effect.

Lord Gardiner, reporting for his commission in 1975, recommended that detention without trial, while arguably effective in the containment of violence, should not remain as a long term policy.

Judge Bennett, an English County Court judge, headed a Committee of Inquiry in 1978 to examine the interrogation practices of the police amidst allegations of use of harsh forms of psychological pressure and physical abuse to extract confessions from suspected terrorists.

Judge Baker issued a report in 1984 that served as a basis for the changes made in the Northern Ireland (Emergency Provisions) Act 1987.

Currently, Lord Colville prepares annual reports on the overall security scheme.

The administration of justice with respect to non-terrorist criminal activity is governed by the Police and Criminal Evidence (NI) Order 1989 (PACE). PACE differs in some respects from the criminal justice codes in effect in England. It is not normally invoked in cases involving alleged acts of terrorism or political crimes.

Police powers under PACE are generally limited by requirements of "cause" and "reasonableness." For example, PACE authorizes the police to arrest any person without a warrant who is reasonably suspected of committing or having committed any one of a range of criminal offenses, or of inciting, aiding, abetting, counselling or procuring their commission. In exercising powers under PACE, the police "may use reasonable force, if necessary." (Article 88).

The Power to Arrest

The Emergency Provisions Act (1991) and the Prevention of Terrorism Act (1989) govern police powers and procedures in the investigation, arrest and detention of persons suspected of terrorist activity. The EPA applies only in Northern Ireland and authorizes broad powers of arrest. Section 17 of the EPA permits the police to "arrest without warrant any person who [the officer] has reasonable grounds to suspect is committing, has committed or is about to commit a scheduled offence or an offence under this Act, which is not a scheduled offence." The scheduled offenses cover a wide range of conduct that could relate to terrorism, including murder, kidnapping, robbery, assault and firearms and explosives violations.[9]

The arrest powers under Section 17 of the EPA are today rarely invoked because the police have even broader arrest and investigative authority under the PTA. Section 14(1) of the PTA permits a police officer to

---

[9] Certain "non-scheduled" offenses are also covered by the Act, including failing to stop and answer questions (Sec. 23(2)), interfering with the power to close roads (Sec. 24(4)), failing to stop a vehicle when required to do so (Sec. 26(10)), and failing to comply with regulations established by the Secretary of State for preserving peace and order (Sec. 58(3)).

arrest without warrant a person whom he has reasonable grounds for suspecting to be

(a) a person guilty of an offense under [certain sections of the PTA which prohibit membership in or support of proscribed organizations, failing to comply with an exclusion order, contributing to acts of terrorism or to the resources of banned organizations];

(b) a person who is or has been concerned in the commission, preparation or instigation of acts of terrorism to which this section applies; or

(c) a person subject to an exclusion order.

The PTA (which applies throughout the United Kingdom) also proscribes certain organizations, subjecting persons in these organizations to criminal penalties.[10] Further, the PTA authorizes exclusion orders, imposed by the Secretary of State for Northern Ireland or the Home Secretary, to bar travel by suspected terrorists within certain areas of the United Kingdom. (See Chapter VII, Freedom of Movement.)

Section 14(1) is the authority generally invoked by the police in arrest situations concerning alleged terrorist activity. It is an extremely broad grant of police power, authorizing arrests for unspecified crimes as long as there is reasonable suspicion of involvement in terrorism. Given the vague definition of terrorism ("the use of violence for political ends, including any use of violence for the purpose of putting the public or any section of the public in fear"), the police have authority to arrest on the most limited suspicion, information or intelligence.

The statistical data relating to the use of this power raise serious questions as to its purpose. From 1974-1989, approximately 10,000 persons were detained under the PTA, but only 30% were actually charged with a criminal offense, and only 1% were charged with a PTA

---

[10] See Chapter VI for the list of proscribed organizations.

offense.[11] These statistics and numerous interviews conducted by the Helsinki Watch mission with persons who have been arrested, detained and interrogated pursuant to the PTA, make it evident that in a significant number of cases the security forces arrest individuals without cause to believe that they are involved in criminal activity. These arrests are in some instances motivated by an interest in gathering intelligence information, persuading the arrested person to become an informer, or simply to harass those believed to be involved in particular political causes.

Interviews conducted with prisoners who have been subjected to arrest under this provision, attorneys involved in the defense of criminal cases, and security officials support the widely expressed view that the arrest power is often invoked for reasons other than criminal investigation:

> * Padraig Wilson, who served six years in prison from 1977-1983 for activities on behalf of the IRA, has been arrested six times over the past seven years, held for interrogation for periods of up to seven days on each occasion, and released each time without criminal charges. In two of these cases, he received compensation from the government for false arrest.

> * Thomas Braniff has been arrested seven times over the past several years, but charged only once with a criminal offense (for which he was acquitted). He claims that he has been threatened and physically abused during the ensuing interrogations. He too was awarded compensation for police abuse.

> * Patrick McDade has been arrested over ten times since 1983 and never charged. He too claims verbal threats during interrogation and efforts to convince him to become an informer.

---

[11] Unpublished manuscript on emergency legislation in Northern Ireland. Liberty (National Council for Civil Liberties), London, 1990. Chapter III, "The Operation of the Prevention of Terrorism Acts in Northern Ireland," p.1.

As discussed in the section on Interrogation, the large majority of criminal prosecutions for terrorist-related offenses involve confessions by the defendant. The ability to secure confessions is enhanced by the broad powers of arrest and by the authority to detain suspects for up to seven days for questioning. The police can arrest for questioning for almost any reason at any time, and with seven days to subject suspects to interrogation, can secure confessions or other police intelligence or persuade detainees to become informers. The powers to arrest and detain are the cornerstone of the security regime in Northern Ireland.[12]

Police Powers to Stop, Search and Seize

In cases involving non-terrorist investigations, the PACE (NI) Order (1989) empowers police officers to stop, detain and search any person in a public place if they have reasonable grounds for suspecting that they will find stolen or prohibited articles. An article is prohibited if it is, for example, an offensive weapon or something intended for use in a burglary or theft. Any such item may be seized and need not be returned.

Under the EPA, the police and army are provided a broad range of powers to stop and search persons and to search residences and other premises. Some of these powers can be exercised without cause or suspicion of criminal activity and all can be exercised without prior judicial approval. Specifically, the following authority is granted by the EPA:

---

[12] Under the EPA, §18, members of the Army may effect an arrest if there is reasonable cause to suspect that the person is committing, has committed or is about to commit an offense. Thereafter, the army may detain and question the suspect for up to four hours, without notice to the suspect's family and without allowing access to a lawyer.

Stops to determine identity or movements

Under §23(1) and §26, the police or army may stop any person or any automobile for the purpose of ascertaining "that persons's identity and movements" and what the person may know "concerning any recent explosion or any other recent incident endangering life . . ." This power to stop and compel answers can be exercised without suspicion. Further, under §19(6)(a), the officer may search the person who has been stopped, to determine if s/he is carrying munitions or transmitters.

Under §20(2) an explosives investigator may stop and search without suspicion any person to ascertain whether that person is carrying explosives.

The police procedure that most frequently has an impact on the citizenry of Northern Ireland is the stopping and searching of pedestrians and automobiles. Given the serious dangers involved in the transportation of explosives, firearms and ammunition in Northern Ireland, a policy of stops and searches if implemented in a fair and neutral manner would not raise questions under international human rights standards. But there is a significant difference between the exercise of the power to stop, question and search a person entering a defined zone or fixed checkpoint, where all persons will be subjected to this police intrusion, and random stops and searches.

There have been many abuses of this power, particularly in places associated with strong Republican support. In these areas, persons are repeatedly stopped, questioned and searched by heavily-armed security personnel in what appears to be either random conduct, with no cause to believe that the individuals are involved in any unlawful activity, or purposeful stops based on the subject's political views or associations. Such army and police patrols are not only offensive to human rights norms,[13] but may be counter-productive from a security viewpoint, since they continue to create antagonism to the overall security operations in Northern Ireland.

---

[13] Both the International Covenant on Civil and Political Rights (1966) (Article 7) and the European Convention on Human Rights (1950) (Article 3) prohibit inhuman or degrading treatment.

The Helsinki Watch mission received many allegations of harassment.

* A Belfast lawyer said that his clients were stopped daily by soldiers and the RUC. "Our clients can't leave their own houses without being stopped three, four or five times, and then followed. Each time they are asked their name and address; then they are stopped 100 yards further down the street by a second patrol and asked the same questions."

* William Smith, the head of "Justice for All," a group formed in 1989 to bring attention to abuses suffered by Loyalists at the hands of security forces, said that the Loyalist community regularly experiences harassment by security forces in the form of street stops and house searches.

* One young man in Belfast who is the subject of an order excluding him from England said that his house was under constant watch and that he has been stopped and searched numerous times in the past year. "They stop me, they search me, they ask me my name, although they know it very well, and they threaten to kill me. Once I had my young son in my arms and the police stopped me and made me comment on a recent IRA incident, and told me to 'watch your back.' The policeman said, 'yes, that is a threat.' In the summer of 1989, a sergeant accused me of being an IRA terrorist, and said he was going to put my photo and description on public notice boards."

* A Sinn Fein councillor in Omagh said that he is stopped regularly by security forces. On December 12, 1990, for example, he was stopped on a main road near his house and kept there for 45 minutes. British soldiers asked for his identification, then told him to take his car off the road; both he and his car were searched thoroughly. He alleges that he was verbally abused and accused of supporting murderers.

17

The next day the councillor was stopped in the same place on the same road and made to go through the same acts. The following week he was held for 15 minutes; on December 19 he was given a warning. He said that being stopped is not at all unusual for him; he estimates that during 1990 he was stopped and held between 50 and 60 times. He has never been charged with an offense; five years ago he was detained briefly for questioning. Two years ago he received a Christmas card wishing him a "happy last Christmas"; mailed in Omagh, it was signed, "the RUC [Royal Ulster Constabulary], the UDR [Ulster Defense Regiment] and the British Army."[14]

* Father Joseph McVeigh, a parish priest in County Fermanagh, said; "I see daily intimidation of young people, really appalling abuse. People are held for hours, insulted, sometimes physically beaten--women as well as men. It happens at checkpoints and also by mobile patrols. Sometimes people are chosen at random, and sometimes people associated with Sinn Fein are targeted. It's been more intense in the past year."

Father McVeigh himself refuses to be searched on the road, and he has been taken to barracks a few times to be searched. "Because I take a strong human rights line I have been labeled Sinn Fein, and have been told that 'terrorists use priests.' There have been times when I felt my life in danger; other priests are in the same situation." At Christmastime he received a Christmas card that said, "Have a good day--it could be your last. Love the boys in green" (the British Army and the UDR wear green uniforms).

---

[14] See Chapter III for a description of the security forces active in Northern Ireland.

*   Father Raymond Murray, a priest in Armagh, said: "They send paratroopers or Marines to South Armagh-- trigger-happy soldiers, bully boys. They're trained for combat; no one can resist them. They stop people and accuse them of being with the IRA, and threaten them. It's been happening a lot the past few months. They frighten the wits out of people. We tell the police, but they don't do anything--they don't charge the army or warn them not to do it.

"The harassment is a lower level of violence, to show you who's in control. If you stand up for your civil rights, they punish you. They stop you and say, 'where are you going? Who are you seeing?' If you won't tell, they make you open the boot of your car. They search it and throw out all the tools and keep you for an hour or so.

"I've been stopped like this six times in the past ten years. A few years ago I was walking in town. A UDR soldier yelled at me, 'Hi, boy.' I passed him by. The next day he did the same thing, but this time stuck his rifle against my throat, pushing my head back, humiliating me on the street."

*   Dr. Joe Hendron, a Social Democratic Labor Party (SDLP) councillor in West Belfast, told Helsinki Watch: "The soldiers think all of West Belfast is their enemy, so they treat the people like muck, like dirt. The biggest factor making people support Sinn Fein and the IRA is their daily confrontation with the security forces. They treat young people like dirt and drive them into the arms of the IRA. There's no place to go with complaints against soldiers. It's very rare for a soldier to be taken to task for his behavior toward civilians."

*   A peace worker in London/Derry told the Helsinki Watch mission of an incident in 1988 in which a friend of his was stopped by soldiers in the rain and made to take off his good jacket, then to take off his shoes and

socks and stand on his jacket. A soldier searched him and, in front of the man's girlfriend, squeezed his testicles and said, "Did you enjoy that?"

* Andrew Puddephat of Liberty (the National Council for Civil Liberties) in London said that their research indicates that many people join paramilitary organizations because of their treatment by security forces on the streets of Northern Ireland.

Chief Constable Hugh Annesley of the Royal Ulster Constabulary (the Northern Ireland police force) told the Helsinki Watch mission that "it would be ludicrous to pretend that soldiers, the UDR and the RUC never make mistakes. But some people tell lies about being harassed, and some come in and out of checkpoints looking for trouble. Most of these cases are minor and difficult, since it's one person's word against another's. We can't provide standard policing in West Belfast--it takes twelve soldiers to protect one constable in some areas. But there has been a steady and incremental improvement in relations between the RUC and the public. The army has improved too; soldiers are not usually trained to deal with people, but now that is changing, and they see that everybody in Northern Ireland is not a villain."

Asked how the government controls low-level harassment by security forces, a spokesperson for the Northern Ireland Office told the Helsinki Watch mission that the answers lie in training and in internal disciplinary procedures. He said that the UDR trains soldiers on how to deal with the public. He also reported that police training emphasizes the need for good relations with the community. He pointed out the harassment security force personnel receive from the public--sometimes verbal and sometimes physical. "Of course, that doesn't wholly excuse security forces' harassment of the public in return," he said. "The response must be proportionate."

A peace worker in London/Derry told the Helsinki Watch mission that the attitude of the local commander of the army makes a great deal of difference in the level of harassment by army troops. He reported that when the commander is sensitive to civilian complaints of harassment the level of abuse drops significantly.

The International Covenant on Civil and Political Rights provides that "No one shall be subjected to torture or to cruel, inhuman or degrading treatment or punishment." (Article 7) The European Convention on Human Rights provides that "No one shall be subjected to torture or to inhuman or degrading treatment or punishment." (Article 3) Based on the reports and discussion above, Helsinki Watch believes that the treatment by security forces in stopping individuals in Northern Ireland to search or question them has on some occasions been degrading. Accordingly, Helsinki Watch recommends that the UK take steps to end random street stops and searches and to ensure that all searches are conducted without degrading or harassing measures.

House Searches

The EPA authorizes searches of premises, including residences (1) to arrest a suspected terrorist (§16); (2) to arrest a person suspected of offenses listed in the Act (§17(2)); (3) to look for explosives, firearms, ammunition or transmitters (§19); and (4) to look for persons who have been kidnapped (§21).

If the place to be searched is a dwelling, under §19 and §21, authority to conduct the search must be granted by a police officer not below the rank of chief inspector, upon a determination that reasonable grounds exist for suspecting the presence of what is being sought.

The procedures used in searching residences raise substantial human rights questions. Under §19 of the EPA, the police may enter and search residences without a judicial warrant if they have reasonable grounds to believe that explosives, weapons or other terrorist contraband is present. Most of the searches are conducted in neighborhoods with Republican loyalties. Further, they are carried out under a strong show of force and often involve the literal tearing apart of a home--walls are removed, floor boards ripped up, ceilings torn down and personal items destroyed.

Invasive searches may be necessary to try to locate arms and explosives that may be hidden in remote areas of a house, but the high number of house searches that do not produce arms or contraband is troublesome. In 1990, the Northern Ireland Information Service tabulated the following information regarding residence searches:

TABLE I

Searches of Premises under s. 15 EPA 1978

Year	Army			RUC
	Occupied	Unoccupied/ Derelict	Total	
1985	104	184	188	N/A
1986	137	207	344	1818
1987	393	232	625	2474
1988	751	556	1307	4136
1989	725	384	1109	3027
1990 1st Quarter	130	133	263	767

Source: Northern Ireland Information Service, Statistics on Northern Ireland Emergency Legislation, issued 31 July 1990.

Statistics regarding the number of searches that produced contraband are not fully available, but those provided by the Northern Ireland Office establish that in recent years the rate of successful searches is in the 5-10% range. The NIO reports that in 1990 army searches of "occupied houses" resulted in "positive searches" in only 34 of 671 search operations.[15] Unless otherwise explained, this extremely low rate of success demonstrates that the police are not acting with reasonable suspicion in conducting these searches. Clearly, if the information provided to the police from informers or other sources was generally credible, we would expect the police to find illegal material more often than not, or at least close to half of the time. The 5.1% rate suggests that the information is largely unfounded, and yet the police continue to justify and implement this massively invasive technique. Simply put, the results do not justify the means, and even if compensation is paid to those whose property is damaged,[16] the violations of law are too pronounced to ignore.[17]

---

[15] The NIO defines "positive searches" as "those resulting in finds of weapons, munitions or illegal radio equipment or of empty hides [i.e., hiding places] constructed for such purposes." The NIO also stated that the figures on house searches *cannot be related* to those detailing arms finds." (Letter from Elizabeth Hume of the NIO, February 5, 1991.)

[16] The Northern Ireland Office provided the Helsinki Watch mission with figures for all compensation paid out by the government under emergency legislation since 1970/71. The NIO said, "It is not possible to distill a figure for compensation paid as a result of house searches for the whole period because the figures are compiled to include the amount which has been paid in respect of land or property requisitioned, damage caused by patrols to fences, crops, etc., and by the cratering of border roads." The total amount of compensation paid out from Fiscal Years 1970/71 through 1990/91 is 6,934,354 pounds. The figure for 1990/91 is 1,750,000 pounds (approximate). Letter from NIO dated 23 April, 1991.

[17] It was suggested to the mission that the disparity in the figures may be explained by a policy that involves searches of numerous houses at the same time to provide "cover" for the house to be targeted and for police informants. This was acknowledged by a government minister in Parliament but later denied. Putting aside the fact that such a policy would itself be illegal (house searches are

(continued...)

Under §19(4) of the EPA, the occupants of a house being searched may be required to stay in one part of the house for up to four hours. This period can be extended for another four hours by a police officer of the rank of superintendent or above. This is, in effect, a form of house arrest, and can greatly increase the anxiety suffered by a person or family subjected to a search, and add to feelings of harassment.

Interviews with persons subjected to the search policies demonstrate the extent to which abuses can occur. Patrick McDade claims that his house was searched eight times since 1983 and that no contraband or other illegal item was found. Padraig Wilson claims that his mother's house has been searched ten times without a finding of contraband. And Seamus Finucane (brother of Patrick Finucane, a lawyer killed by loyalist para-militaries) claims ten searches, all with negative results.

Further representations were made to the mission:

* A lawyer who represents both Loyalists and Republicans in the London/Derry area, said that he knew of at least 50 house searches of his clients' homes (with nothing seized); most of his clients do not file complaints about the searches.

* William Smith, of Justice for All, a group in West Belfast that is concerned with abuses of the Unionist community, told the mission he knew of hundreds of house searches during the previous year. He believes that more Protestant houses have been searched recently; security forces are "bending over backwards to show

_____

^{17}(...continued)
authorized only upon "reasonable grounds" that illegal material will be discovered), the policy hardly serves legitimate interests since the community will soon know from where the contraband was seized. Moreover, there is an obvious price paid in terms of community outrage and resentment for unsuccessful searches.

they're non-sectarian." He said that the Justice for All office had been searched as well.

* A Sinn Fein councillor in Omagh said that his house had been "raided" in February, 1990. His wife and children were confined to one room in the house while security forces searched the house for two and a half hours.

* A member of the Ulster Defense Association, a Loyalist paramilitary group, said that his house was searched three times in 1989. Another UDA member said his house had been searched in his absence and left open. A third said his house had been searched twice in three weeks in 1988, and twice in 1990.

* A merchant seaman in North Belfast gave the mission details of a destructive search of his home that took place in October 1989. The seaman lives alone. Six hours before the search, in the early evening, he heard gunfire and when he opened the back door he saw a badly wounded police officer. Two men then jumped the seaman, put a gun to his head and told him to get out of there. After the gunmen left, the seaman went to the front of his house, where he found a constable and told him of the incident. Police then came to the back of his house and took away the body of the officer. They told the seaman "we'll be back to look around." The seaman went to his girlfriend's house for the night.

That night the seaman's house was searched. A neighbor reported that he heard the seaman's door being broken down at about 1:00 a.m., and "the clip of a gun." The police were there for about 15 minutes and, on leaving, told the neighbor that they "had to do a little damage."

Not long afterwards, soldiers in jeeps arrived and entered the seaman's house. They stayed for three and a half hours, completely gutting the house, leaving clothes strewn about, camera and TV smashed, the fireplace ripped out, and carpets ripped from the floor. The seaman counted 27 holes in his walls from the search.

The seaman told the mission that he had been afraid to go to the police; instead, he went to a solicitor, who talked with the NIO. The NIO sent someone to look at the seaman's house, and found it, as the seaman had said, unlivable. An assessor then came and offered the seaman 3,000 pounds in compensation, telling him to take it or leave it. Although the seaman believed that this amount was far less than the cost of the damage, which he estimated at 6,000 pounds, he took the money because Christmas was coming and he was afraid that pipes would freeze and destroy the house.

Lord Colville, who has been charged for several years with reviewing the emergency legislation for Parliament, told the Helsinki Watch mission that house searches were appropriate because, although "a fair number turn up nothing, a fair number turn up something." He believes searches are done on the basis of careful intelligence work, and that the search powers are necessary for security forces to find firearms and explosives. In his 1990 review, he recommended no change in the house search powers set out in the EPA.

Helsinki Watch concludes that the power to search houses and the manner in which it is done are improper; a search of a house or other premises and the removal of documents or other property should be made only under court supervision. A warrant should be required for such searches. Helsinki Watch believes that the search and entry powers set out in the PACE Order are adequate and recommends that the EPA search and entry powers be repealed.[18]

---

[18] Under the Emergency Provisions Act 1991, a constable or a soldier can, *without* reasonable suspicion, "examine any document or record found in the course of the search for ascertaining whether it contains any . . . information" regarding certain groups of persons, including policemen, soldiers, judges, court

(continued...)

The Power to Detain

The maximum period of ordinary detention without charge is 24 hours. (PACE, Article 42(1)). Detention beyond 24 hours is permissible only for "serious arrestable offenses," including offenses under the PTA. In these cases a police officer of at least the rank of superintendent may authorize detention for an additional 12 hours, provided there are reasonable grounds for believing that this detention is necessary to secure evidence and that the investigation is being conducted diligently and expeditiously. (Article 43(1)). In normal criminal investigations, therefore, the police may detain a person without charge for up to 36 hours.

Detention beyond 36 hours is allowed only if authorized by a magistrates' court. The court can initially permit detention for an additional 36 hours. A second court order can be applied for, but the total period of detention from the time of the arrest may not exceed 96 hours (Articles 44 and 45).

Persons arrested under section 14(1) of the PTA are subject to detention and interrogation procedures far different from those authorized for arrests under PACE and the EPA. Under the PTA, the arrestee can be detained for up to 48 hours after arrest and for up to an additional five days upon authorization by the Secretary of State. The power to hold and question a suspect for up to seven days raises serious human rights issues. Some of these will be discussed below with respect to the interrogation policies and practices that are employed during the detention period, but even absent interrogation the lengthy detention without charge or judicial authorization is a violation of international human rights standards. In *Brogan v. United Kingdom* (1988), the European Court of Human Rights ruled that a detention under the PTA that exceeded four days and six hours violated Article 5(3) of the

---

[18](...continued)
officials and prison officers. Helsinki Watch believes that a warrant should be required for examining or seizing documents.

European Convention on Human Rights. In response, the United Kingdom has "derogated" from that section of the Convention, rather than reforming its detention practices.[19]

Over the years detention has been extended beyond the initial 48 hour period in more than half the cases, as the following table shows.

---

[19] Explaining the UK's decision to derogate from the ECHR, then-Home Secretary David Waddington on November 14, 1989, stated that the government believed it necessary to retain the power to detain terrorist suspects for up to seven days, and would not introduce a "new judicial element" to authorize such detention. The Home Secretary said that decisions to detain suspects "may be, and often are, taken on the basis of information, the nature and source of which could not be revealed to a suspect or his legal adviser without serious risk to individuals helping the police or the prospect of further valuable intelligence being lost." He added that to allow a court to make a decision on information which a detainee had not seen would be "a radical departure from the principles which govern judicial proceedings in this country and could seriously affect public trust and confidence in the independence of the judiciary." The legality of the decision to derogate is now before the European Court of Human Rights in the cases of *Peter Brannigan v. UK*, Application No. 14553/89, and *Patrick McBride v. UK*, Application No. 14554/89,

TABLE II

Detentions Under the Prevention of Terrorism Acts or Supplemental Orders 1974, 1976, 1984 and 1989 in Northern Ireland[20]

Year	Persons Detained	Extension of Detention Granted
1974	-	-
1975	8	5
1976	246	202
1977	162	123
1978	151	144
1979	162	126
1980	222	186
1981	495	401
1982	828	639
1983	1175	728
1984	908	533
1985	938	557
1986	1309	484
1987	1459	451
1988	1717	542
1989	843 (up to 30 June 1989)	238
Total	10,627	5,359

----

[20] Northern Ireland Information Service, "Prevention of Terrorism Act."

Internment

The practice of internment (detaining persons for indefinite periods of time without judicial authorization) was adopted as part of the EPA in 1973. Under this section of the emergency laws, the Secretary of State can make an interim custody order for the temporary detention of any person. Within 28 days the matter must be referred to a non-judicial commission for a determination of whether the person had been engaged in terrorism and whether detention is necessary for the protection of the public. Internment under this procedure is for an indefinite time. Detention orders have not been executed since 1975, but the authority to do so continues. Again, international standards of human rights condemn this procedure[21] and many independent observers, as well as Lord Colville, have urged its termination. Helsinki Watch recommends that the power to intern without judicial authorization be repealed.

Interrogation

Confessions play a major part in the criminal justice system in Northern Ireland. In a 1981 study, Dermott Walsh found that confessions were involved in 89% of all scheduled offense cases.[22] The heavy reliance on confessions has continued since that study; the CAJ

---

[21] Article 9 of the International Covenant on Civil and Political Rights provides:

3. Anyone arrested or detained on a criminal charge shall be brought promptly before a judge or other officer authorized by law to exercise judicial power and shall be entitled to trial within a reasonable time or to release. . . .

4. Anyone who is deprived of his liberty by arrest or detention shall be entitled to take proceedings before a court, in order that that court may decide without delay on the lawfulness of his detention and order his release if the detention is not lawful.

Article 4(3) and (4) of the European Convention on Human Rights contains the same protections in almost identical language.

[22] Walsh, *The Use and Abuse of Emergency Legislation in Northern Ireland.* Cobden Trust, 1983.

believes that the percentage has not significantly changed since that time.[23] Accordingly, from a human rights perspective, it is critical to ensure that confessions are not the product of improper police conduct and that the legal standards for admissibility are sufficiently rigorous to exclude confessions that are obtained with undue pressure or are otherwise unreliable.

An important limitation on police interrogation practices is reflected in the traditional rule that only "voluntary" statements can be introduced into evidence against the accused. Under this standard, the prosecution has the burden of demonstrating that the statement was not obtained "by fear of prejudice or hope of advantage held out by a person in authority" and that the statement was not obtained by "oppression." Judges' Rules, 1964, para. 3.

The EPA substantially reduced the protections afforded an accused during interrogation. Under the original EPA, a statement obtained by the police was admissible unless the defendant produced *prima facie* evidence that he "was subjected to torture or to inhuman or degrading treatment in order to induce him to make the statement." (§8, EPA (1973)).

The conflict between this legislation and the long- established common law rules led to confusion in judicial determinations and to an increase in harsh abuses of suspects.

Some courts admitted confessions during this period even where there was evidence of physical abuse. In *R. v. McCormick*, (1977) N.I. 105, Lord Justice McGonigal wrote that §6 (now §11):

> appears to accept a degree of physical violence which could never be tolerated by the courts under the common law test and if the words in section 6 are to be construed in the same sense as the words used in Article 3 (of the European Convention for the Protection of Human Rights and Fundamental Freedoms), it leaves open to an interviewer to use a moderate degree of

---

[23] Committee on the Administration of Justice. *A Briefing Paper on the Northern Ireland (Emergency Provisions) Bill*, December 1990, p. 15.

physical maltreatment for the purpose of inducing a person to make a statement.[24]

Moreover, the courts permitted psychological pressure by the authorities, admitting confessions made in response to threats or inducements.

In 1984, Amnesty International reviewed this area and stated:

> The law regarding the admissibility in evidence of statements made by a suspect in police custody has been fundamentally altered. Involuntary statements are legally admissible evidence, unless induced by torture, or by inhuman or degrading treatment. This change has not only obviated "technical" legal requirements, but has also removed from the law on admissibility the basic function of minimizing the risk that unreliable statements are brought before the tribunal of fact.

> * * *

> Nonetheless (and contrary to Lord Diplock's proposals), the courts have retained a discretion to exclude evidence on the grounds that its "prejudicial effect outweighs its probative value and to admit the evidence would not be in the interests of justice."

> It would appear that the courts usually exercise this discretion to exclude confessions apparently obtained as a result of physical maltreatment falling short of torture, inhuman or degrading treatment. Beyond this, there is

---

[24] Not all courts agreed. See *R. v. O'Halloran*, (1979) 2 NIJB (CA): This Court finds it difficult to envisage any form of physical violence which is relevant to the interrogation of a suspect in custody and which, if it had occurred, could at the same time leave a court satisfied beyond reasonable doubt in relation to the issue for decision under section 6.

no consistent judicial practice, but neither statements obtained as a result of repeated, prolonged and forceful questioning, nor statements obtained as a result of threats or promises are as a rule excluded.[25]

The Bennett Committee documented the abuses in the interrogation process and recommended changes in procedure. These included the closed-circuit TV monitoring of all interrogations, full documentation of all aspects of a suspect's treatment while in custody, regular provisions of food and water, and medical examinations for all persons brought into custody.

It appears that until quite recently the stark physical abuses that attended interrogations during the 1970's had abated, but the reforms implemented as a result of the Bennett Committee and other studies have not ended human rights violations.[26] As one commentator has written:

> For a start it would appear that they are not being fully followed in practice. Closed circuit television cameras have been installed, medical examinations are being offered and accepted, detectives are undergoing a training programme, a new code of conduct has been introduced and records are being maintained. But the recommendations on the number of detectives involved in any one interrogation and in any one case, on access to a solicitor and on the length of interrogation sessions are not being fully complied with. It would also seem that the code is not being strictly followed as many suspects are claiming that they are being subjected to verbal abuse and to pressure being applied on them to act as informers. Furthermore, the closed-circuit

---

[25] Korff, *The Diplock Courts in Northern Ireland, a Fair Trial*, at 60, 61.

[26] See Appendix A for recent interviews by the Committee on the Administration of Justice in Belfast with three men who allege mistreatment during detention. See also Amnesty International's June 1991 report, "United Kingdom: Human Rights Concerns," which documents serious allegations of ill-treatment in detention.

television cameras are not always switched on, and, when they are, they are monitored by uniformed RUC officers.[27]

Criticism of existing practices led to a revision of the EPA in 1987. Under §11, a "threat of violence" is now grounds for exclusion of a confession. Further, the courts now have express discretion to exclude statements in the interests of fairness to the accused or in the interests of justice.

Unfortunately, legislative reforms have not been sufficient to ensure compliance by the security forces with human rights standards. Instances of physical abuse, harassment, and threats have been documented and, with the continued heavy reliance on confessions in the prosecution of terrorist crime, Helsinki Watch lacks confidence in the procedures that are currently used to obtain confessions.[28]

Closed circuit tv monitoring has proved of little help in resolving allegations of abuse. A more effective deterrent to abuse would be video and audio tape-recording of interrogations. The Standing Advisory Commission on Human Rights for Northern Ireland has called for video recording. In his 1990 review, Lord Colville, too, recommended that silent video tapes be kept. Lord Colville also suggested that experiments

---

[27] Walsh, *The Use and Abuse of Emergency Legislation in Northern Ireland, supra,* at 77 (quoted in *Criminal Justice and Human Rights in Northern Ireland, A Report to the Association of the Bar of the City of New York,* William E. Hellerstein, Robert B. McKay and Peter R. Schlam, 1983).

[28] See specific cases detailed below. It has been suggested that the increase in the number of complaints concerning interrogation abuses is a result of the increased emphasis the police have put on confessions following the demise of the "Supergrass" trials. In the early 1980's many significant cases were prosecuted on the word of former terrorists, turned informers (called "Supergrasses"). Supergrass convictions were controversial because they were based on the uncorroborated testimony of accomplices who were given immunity or short sentences for their crimes. Ultimately, many of the convictions obtained in this manner were reversed in the appellate courts. See, *Civil Liberties in Northern Ireland, the CAJ Handbook,* Belfast, 1990, p. 55.

be conducted in Northern Ireland into audio recording summaries of interviews with "suspected terrorists."[29]

One argument against audio recording is that suspects might be less willing to volunteer "off the record" information in the fear that it might later be disclosed by the police, which could lead to retribution by paramilitary groups. That risk is already present with any statement by a person interrogated by the police, but it is easier to deny the validity of a statement that has not been recorded. The risk of retaliation against a suspect must be weighed against the benefits to be gained by a video- and audio-recording system that would document the treatment accorded to a suspect in detention.

Given the substantial number of complaints of abuse under the present system of closed-circuit tv monitoring, Helsinki Watch recommends that video- and audio-recording be implemented, at least on a trial basis, under strict regulations against unwarranted disclosure. Helsinki Watch also recommends that detainees' attorneys have access to all video- and audio-recordings of interrogations.

In addition to the abuses discussed above, it is important in assessing the interrogation process to consider as well the coercion that can result by virtue of the lengthy time allowed for interrogation and the incommunicado aspects of the system. As discussed above, under §14 of the PTA a "terrorist" suspect can be interrogated for up to 48 hours without the right to consult with a solicitor. If a request to speak with counsel is made during the first 48 hours it can be denied if a senior RUC officer determines that the exercise of this right will lead to interference with witnesses or evidence or the alerting of other suspects, or will hinder the recovery of property or proceeds of a crime. This provision is frequently invoked in investigations into

---

[29] *Review of the Northern Ireland (Emergency Provisions) Acts 1978 and 1987*, Viscount Colville of Culross, Q.C. ("Colville Report"). London: July 1990. Paragraph 4.9.

terrorist acts. For example, for the years 1987-1989, approximately 60 percent of the requests for legal advice were delayed.[30]

Furthermore, even where counsel is permitted access to a suspect, the interview may be monitored by officials if the supervisory official at the interrogation center determines that such monitoring is necessary to prevent undue interference with the investigation process.[31] If the detention period is extended beyond the 48 hour period, a solicitor may be permitted to see the client only once every 48 hours. A solicitor is never allowed to be present during official interrogation.

Interrogations can continue for up to seven consecutive days upon the approval of the Secretary of State. Where a suspect is kept virtually isolated from the outside world, without criminal charges or access to a court, and is subjected to the sophisticated questioning of teams of detectives, there is a substantial question whether any resulting confession can be deemed voluntary. Surely it is exceedingly difficult to assess this issue months later at a judicial proceeding. The inherent pressure brought to bear by these circumstances militates strongly against extended interrogations.

Many persons complained to the Helsinki Watch mission about extended interrogation and a significant number raised specific allegations of brutality:[32]

> * Brian Gillen was arrested in 1987 and interrogated concerning a killing of a police officer. He was physically abused and suffered a punctured eardrum, a

---

[30] Unpublished manuscript on emergency legislation in Northern Ireland. Liberty (the National Council for Civil Liberties), London, 1990. Chapter I, "The Emergency Provisions Legislation," p. 17.

[31] Lawyers in Northern Ireland confirmed to the mission that such monitoring occurs: a Belfast solicitor reported that police listen in on his legal consultations. A lawyer in London/Derry reported that inspectors sat in on one out of every ten or fifteen of his interviews with clients.

[32] In addition, see Appendix A.

condition that was diagnosed by a doctor at the interrogation center. Gillen alleged that he was threatened throughout the interrogation process, that he was told that his lawyer was associated with the IRA and was only "in it for the money," and that he (Gillen) should become an informer. A court found that there was a *prima facie* case that Gillen had been assaulted and before a full hearing took place the RUC released him.

* Martin McSheffrey stated that during his detention and interrogation in October, 1989, he was hit on the ears and painfully cuffed at the wrists. He stated that he signed a statement acknowledging possession of explosives the next day because he was afraid of getting the "wrist treatment" again. A doctor examined him and found blood clots in his eardrum. The Court threw out the confession and McSheffrey was acquitted.

* Brian Austin states that during his detention in January, 1989 and again in November, 1989 he was threatened with physical injury and death and was subjected to minor physical abuse. He was released without charges.

* Thomas Braniff alleges that he was seriously abused during interrogation in March, 1988, and April, 1989 and that he was awarded compensation for the 1988 arrest.

* Thomas Hughes was arrested and interrogated on four different occasions in 1990. He was told that "loyalists would get him" unless he cooperated. He was released on each occasion without charges.

* Patrick McBride was arrested in March 1990. He claims physical injuries caused by the police during interrogation. He has brought his case to the European Court challenging the United Kingdom's derogation from the European Convention with respect to the length of detention. The case is pending.

* Ciaran Doherty was arrested and detained twice in 1990 and claims both verbal and physical abuse. He also claims (as do many of the others who complained of abuses during interrogation) that he has been subjected to regular harassment by security forces (street stops, searches, etc.).

* Serious allegations of false and fabricated confessions have also been made in the case of the "UDR Four," which concerns the murder convictions of four members of the Ulster Defense Regiment in a sectarian killing. This case is particularly troublesome since the defendants were themselves security officers who, one might assume, would be far less intimidated in the interrogation setting. If these men were in fact coerced, other allegations of abuse gain credence.

The recent release of the Birmingham Six from prison in England after 17 years is sobering evidence of the serious potential for abuse involved in the use of confessions, particularly in high profile cases involving terrorist crimes. There is now undisputed proof that the confessions of these men were either coerced or fabricated and that the conspiracy to frame them was widespread within the security system. The failure of the English courts to review this case in a timely manner raises strong doubts about the police and judicial procedures in England concerning interrogation, and suggests that the interrogation process in Northern Ireland may reflect similar problems.

The attitude of some officials may be reflected in the extraordinary opinion of Lord Denning in 1980 rejecting a civil suit alleging police misconduct in the Birmingham Six cases:

Just consider the course of events if this action were to proceed to trial. It will not be tried for 18 months or two years. It will take weeks and weeks. The evidence about violence and threats will be given all over again, but this time six or seven years after the event, instead of one year. If the six men fail, it will mean that much time and money and worry will have been expended by many people for no good purpose. If the six men win, it will mean that the police were guilty of perjury, that they were guilty of violence and threats, that the confessions were involuntary and were improperly admitted in evidence, and that the convictions were erroneous. That would mean that the Home Secretary would have either to recommend they be pardoned or he would have to remit the case to the Court of Appeals under §17 of the Criminal Appeal Act 1968. This is such an appalling vista that every sensible person in the land would say: "It cannot be right that these actions should go any further."

. . .

This case shows what a civilized country we are. Here are six men who have been proved guilty of the most wicked murder of 21 innocent people. They have no money. Yet the state lavished large sums on their defense. They were convicted of murder and sentenced to imprisonment for life. In their evidence they were guilty of gross perjury. Yet the state continued to lavish large sums on them, in their actions against the police. It is high time that it stopped. It is really an attempt to set aside the convictions by sidewind. It is a scandal that it should be allowed to continue.[33]

Helsinki Watch has concluded that the standard for admissibility of confessions in Diplock Courts in Northern Ireland permits the admission into evidence of unreliable confessions and violates the right of defendants to a fair trial. There is also a substantial question as to whether the EPA standard for admissibility of confessions meets the standard set in the International Covenant on Civil and Political Rights, to which the UK is a signatory. Article 14(3) requires that

[i]n the determination of any criminal charge against him, everyone shall be entitled to the following minimum guarantees, in full equality:

---

[33] *McIlkeny v. Chief Constable*, 2 AllER, 239-40 (1982).

. . . (g) not to be compelled to testify against himself or
to confess guilt.

Helsinki Watch recommends that the PACE standard for admissibility of confessions should apply in scheduled offense cases, as well as in non-scheduled cases, and that the EPA standard be abolished.

Helsinki Watch recommends that detainees have immediate and regular access to attorneys, that detainees be brought before a court within 48 hours of detention, and that the UK repeal its derogation from Article (5)(3) of the European Convention on Human Rights.

The Right to Silence

The right of an accused person to remain silent has been a major part of English law for over 300 years. In 1988 this right was fundamentally changed in Northern Ireland by the enactment of the Criminal Evidence (NI) Order. The Order permits a court to consider a suspect's silence in four situations:

* when a defendant offers for the first time during trial an explanation that could reasonably have been expected to have been given during questioning;

* when an accused refuses to explain certain forensic evidence;

* when an accused refuses to account for his or her presence at a particular place; and

* when a defendant remains silent after a case to answer has been made by the prosecution at trial and the defendant has been warned that s/he will be called to give evidence.

The 1988 Order is premised upon several assumptions about a suspect's silence during interrogation or at trial: that silence (1) often is proof of guilt, (2) gives the defense an unfair advantage at trial, and (3) protects the guilty and is an unnecessary right for the innocent.

These assumptions are highly debatable and the empirical evidence on the questions is inconclusive.[34] For example, silence may be invoked to conceal personal or embarrassing information, but not criminal conduct, or it may be invoked out of a concern that the police will unfairly use or distort any disclosures. Further, concerns about a defense "ambush" of the prosecution at trial (by asserting a defense not disclosed by answers to questions by the police) are adequately met by pre-trial notice and discovery procedures. Assertion of defenses of alibi or insanity can be predicated on pre-trial notice. Disclosure of defense witnesses can be required in a system of mutual pre-trial discovery.

More important, in our view, is the role that the right to silence plays in an adversarial system of criminal justice. The right to silence is integral to the presumption of innocence and to the state's burden to prove guilt beyond a reasonable doubt. In an adversarial system the state may not compel the defendant to become an agent of the prosecution. Voluntary statements and testimony are admissible, but *compelled* testimony is not. To allow adverse comment and inferences to flow from the invocation of the right to silence is largely to abrogate the right itself.

In the context of the emergency criminal justice provisions in effect in Northern Ireland, it is particularly inadvisable to provide the police with yet another tool to undermine an individual's determination to remain silent. It should be recalled that in Northern Ireland one can be detained and questioned for up to seven days on the vaguest of grounds--suspicion of terrorism--with strictly limited access to counsel. If one is charged with a "terrorist offense" there is no right to trial by jury. These emergency laws have made deep inroads on traditional protections for the accused. In such a system, the right to silence is an important human liberty.[35]

---

[34] See, e.g., *The Right of Silence*, James Wood and Adam Crawford (Civil Liberties Trust, 1989).

[35] This is not to say that the right to silence is an immutable condition of a fair criminal justice system. Inquisitorial systems, which place the burden of questioning of witnesses, including suspects, on a neutral magistrate (in the presence of counsel), and which protect a suspect from custodial police
(continued...)

Moreover, the nature of the advice that is provided to the suspect presents questions that cannot fairly be assessed by the lay person without the advice and assistance of counsel.[36] It will not be clear to a suspect,

---

[35](...continued)
interrogation, allow adverse inferences to be drawn from silence where evidence would normally call for a response. We do not suggest that this procedure offends international human rights standards.

[36] The Criminal Evidence (Northern Ireland) Order 1988 provides three cautions to be given to suspects. The first is under Article 3, and is intended to deal with "ambush defences":
> You do not have to say anything, unless you wish to do so, but I must warn you that if you fail to mention any fact which you wish to rely on in your defence in Court your failure to take this opportunity to mention it may be taken as supporting any relevant evidence against you. If you wish to say anything, what you say may be given in evidence.

The second is under Article 5, and relates to failure to account for objects or marks:
> You do not have to say anything unless you wish to do so but what you may say may be given in evidence. On (date) at (place) a (object) was found on your person/in or on your clothing or footwear/in your possession/ in (place) where you were at the time/a mark was found on such an object, that is (describe mark)/and I have reason to believe that this was attributable to your participation in an offence of (name offence). I therefore request you to account for this (object or mark). I must warn you that if you fail or refuse to do so a Court, Judge or Jury may draw such inferences from your failure or refusal as appear proper.

The third is under Article 6, relating to failure to account for presence at a relevant place.
> You do not have to say anything unless you wish to do so but what you say may be given in evidence. On (date) at (place) about the time the (offence) is alleged to have been committed I have reason to believe your presence at that time may be attributable to your participation in the commission of that offence. I therefore request you to account for your presence at (place) at that time. I must warn you that if you fail or
(continued...)

for example, what is meant by the warning that "the failure to. . . mention. . .any fact you wish to rely on in your defence in Court. . .may be taken as supporting any relevant evidence against you." How is the suspect to know at this point what s/he will rely upon at trial? What is the "relevant evidence" against the suspect? And how can one, at the arrest stage, without counsel or necessary investigation, make any judgment about how the case might be tried?

International human rights law protects the rights of persons appearing before courts and tribunals. Article 14 (3)(g) of the International Covenant on Civil and Political Rights provides that:

(3) In the determination of any criminal charge against him, everyone shall be entitled to the following minimum guarantees, in full equality:
. . .

(g) Not be be compelled to testify against himself or to confess guilt.

Helsinki Watch believes that the Criminal Evidence Order unjustifiably erodes the right to silence. There is no persuasive evidence that limits on this important right are warranted by considerations of law enforcement or public safety. If the procedures regarding pre-trial interrogation were changed to permit full and fair opportunity for consultation with counsel, comment upon the assertion of the right to silence might be appropriate in some circumstance. Short of such a major change in current procedure, the right to silence should be safeguarded. Accordingly, Helsinki Watch recommends that the Criminal Evidence (N.I.) Order be abolished.

---

[36](...continued)
    refuse to do so a Court, Judge or Jury may draw such inferences from your failure or refusal as appear proper.

III. THE USE OF LETHAL FORCE BY SECURITY FORCES

Between 1969 and 1990, security forces in Northern Ireland shot and killed 339 people in connection with political unrest. Over the years, questions have been raised as to whether these deaths represent a "shoot-to-kill" policy on the part of the United Kingdom, an allegation that has been vigorously denied by the UK. In addition, the standard for the use of lethal force by security forces -- "such force as is reasonable in the circumstances" -- has been criticized as being too vague and too weak to deter the use of such force.

The Helsinki Watch mission examined the use of lethal force by security officers in Northern Ireland and the international legal standards for the use of such force.   The mission concluded that the "reasonableness" standard provides too much leeway for the use of deadly force and leads inevitably to abuses. Helsinki Watch believes that the standard for the use of lethal force should be "absolute necessity" and that such force should be used only in proportion to the actual danger presented.

Security Forces in Northern Ireland

The security forces in Northern Ireland are the Royal Ulster Constabulary (RUC) (the Northern Ireland police force), units of the British Army, and the Ulster Defense Regiment (UDR), a locally-recruited regiment of the British Army consisting of part- and full-time members.

Following rioting and violence in London/Derry in 1969, units of the British Army were sent to Northern Ireland, and the government created an advisory committee under Lord Hunt to study the problems of policing in Northern Ireland. In his report, Lord Hunt made five recommendations:

> * Police and military roles should be separate, as in the rest of the United Kingdom.
>
> * The RUC should be relieved of all military duties and should normally be unarmed.

* The B Specials (the Ulster Special Constabulary which had been heavily criticized as being an exclusively Protestant force policing in a discriminatory fashion) should be disbanded.

* An RUC reserve should be formed.

* A new part-time military force should be locally recruited to come under the control of the General Officer Commanding (GOC) Northern Ireland.[37]

As a result of these recommendations, the Ulster Defense Regiment (UDR) was formed. The role of the army was to protect the border and the State against armed attack and sabotage; the role of the UDR was to support the regular army by undertaking guard duties, carrying out patrols and establishing checkpoints and road blocks, particularly in rural areas. The UDR is not deployed for crowd control or riot duties. Both the regular army and the UDR "provide military support for the RUC."[38]

At its highest point in 1972, the British Army numbered 22,000 in the province. On January 31, 1991, the Northern Ireland Office reported that 10,657 regular army troops were stationed in Northern Ireland. Peter Brooke, Secretary of State for Northern Ireland, has stated that "The UK has of course no vested interest in maintaining these high force levels longer than is necessary. . . . This kind of high military profile was made necessary by violence, will be maintained as long as there is violence, but will certainly be reduced when violence comes to an end."[39]

---

[37] *The Ulster Defense Regiment* (Information Pack). Northern Ireland Office, November 1990, p. 1.

[38] *Ibid.*

[39] Speech to businessmen in London, November 9, 1990.

Between 1969 and 1989, 422 army troops lost their lives in Northern Ireland.[40]

In addition to the regular army, 6,074 members of the Ulster Defense Regiment, some full- and some part-time, were on duty in Northern Ireland on December 31, 1990. Between 1970 and November 2, 1990, 189 members and 44 former members of the UDR, a total of 233 UDR soldiers, were killed by paramilitaries.[41]

As of January 31, 1991, the RUC had a force of 8,249 men and women and an additional reserve force of 4,545 officers. Between 1969 and December 1989, 266 RUC officers lost their lives in connection with political unrest.[42]

Of the 76 deaths related to political unrest in 1990, 27 were members of security forces, 45 were civilians, and 4 were paramilitaries.

Fatal Shootings by Security Forces

According to the Irish Information Partnership, security forces killed 329 people between 1969 and 1989, or 11.8 percent of the total number of deaths associated with political unrest. Of these, over half, 178 (54 percent), were civilians with no known connections to paramilitary groups--149 were Catholics, 25 Protestants and 4 other. One hundred twenty-three (37.4 percent) were Republican paramilitaries, and 13 (4 percent) were Loyalist paramilitaries. Another 15 (4.6 percent) were themselves security force members (see Table III). Security forces killed another ten people during 1990, bringing the total killings to 339.

---

[40] RUC Chief Constable's Annual Report for 1989, page 57.

[41] *The Ulster Defense Regiment*, Information Pack. Northern Ireland Office, November 1990, page B-1.

[42] RUC Chief Constable's Annual Report for 1989, page 57.

TABLE   III

Irish Information Partnership: Category B: Violence, Terrorism, Military, Paramilitary, Security and Police Affairs
Tables B1: Summary of Fatal Casualties in Northern Ireland, 1969 to 1989

	Agency Responsible					
Status of Victim	Security Forces	Nationalist Paramilitaries	Loyalist Paramilitaries	Other & Unidentified	Total	Percentage of Total
Security Forces	15	847	10	4	876	31.64
Nationalist Paramilitaries	123	144	21	6	296	10.62
Loyalist Paramilitaries	13	18	40	2	73	2.62
Civilians: Cath	149	173	506	74	902	32.38
Prot	25	379	114	57	575	20.64
Other	4	22	12	1	35	1.40
Civilian total	178	574	632	132	1,516	54.41
Prison Officers	0	23	2	0	25	0.90
Total	329	1,608	705	146	2,786	
Percentage of Total	11.81	57.72	25.31	5.17	100.00	

47

Allegations of a "Shoot to Kill" Policy and the Government's Response

Over the years, there have been allegations that security forces in Northern Ireland have a "shoot to kill" policy. An international lawyers' inquiry into the lethal use of firearms by the security forces in Northern Ireland entitled *Shoot to Kill?* reported in 1985 that:

> The evidence we have heard leads us to conclude that an administrative practice has been allowed to develop in Northern Ireland, by which killings in violation of the European Convention and the International Covenant are at least tolerated, if not actually encouraged. Undercover units of the British Army and the RUC are trained to shoot to kill even where killing is not legally justifiable and where alternative tactics could and should be used. Such administrative practices are illegal in domestic and international law. They should be stopped and training for them should be discontinued immediately.[43]

Father Raymond Murray, a parish priest in Armagh, told the Helsinki Watch mission that security forces have killed 150 people in "unjust killings" since 1969, including the plastic bullet deaths. In his 1990 book, *The SAS in Ireland*, Father Murray details the circumstances surrounding these killings, and charges that the SAS (the British Army Special Air Services Regiment, an elite unit charged with intelligence gathering and surveillance) shot dead 31 people in Northern Ireland between 1981 and 1989, as well as three people in Gibraltar in March 1988:

> *Shoot-to-Kill.* Assassination as administrative policy is not new in Northern Ireland. The 1980's, however, brought it to the level of a campaign. Any IRA member or suspected IRA member found in a compromising situation was to be executed. So that "Ulsterisation"

---

[43] Kadar Asmal, *Shoot to Kill? International Lawyers' Inquiry into the Lethal Use of Firearms by the Security Forces in Northern Ireland.* Mercier Press, Dublin, 1985. Page 134.

would be complete, a special RUC unit was trained by the SAS in their skills in order to eventually replace the SAS units in Northern Ireland. The SAS was brought into full action again after the RUC Special Support Unit and MI5 blundered in shooting dead six unarmed men and seriously wounding a seventh in three separate incidents in County Armagh in 1982. In the period 1981-89 the SAS, aided by RUC intelligence and sometimes accompanied by RUC personnel, has shot dead 31 people in Northern Ireland. On 6 March 1988 the SAS shot dead three IRA members in Gibraltar. The "Shoot-to-Kill" policy became more ruthless after the Brighton Grand Hotel bombing of October 1984 when the IRA attempted to kill the Prime Minister, Mrs. Margaret Thatcher, during the Conservative Party annual conference.[44]

Father Murray told the mission that he believes that killings by security forces fall into three categories. The first are deliberate, professional killings by SAS troops who target IRA men. The second are killings by "trigger-happy bully boys" who harass people and create violent situations that sometimes end in shootings. The third are cases of collusion, in which security forces pass information to paramilitaries, who then shoot and kill suspected terrorists.

The Northern Ireland Office and the United Kingdom have consistently and vigorously denied that a "shoot to kill" policy exists. In December 1990, the British Information Service provided the Helsinki Watch mission with a leaflet entitled, "Human Rights in Northern Ireland," which states:

> There is no "shoot to kill" policy in Northern Ireland. The law provides that "any person may use such force as is reasonable in the circumstances in the prevention of crime, or in effecting or assisting in the lawful arrest of offenders or suspected offenders." The police and army

---

[44] Raymond Murray, *The SAS in Ireland*. Mercier Press, Dublin, 1990. Page 31.

are issued with specific instructions on opening fire, designed to keep them wholly within the law, and it is made clear, in particular, that firearms must only be used as a last resort. Like everyone else, the security forces must obey the law and are answerable to the courts for their actions.

A spokesperson for the Northern Ireland Office told us that "the primary goal of the security forces is to eradicate the terrorism that has cost nearly 3,000 lives in twenty years." He strongly denied that there is a shoot to kill policy. He emphasized the danger for police in West Belfast; he said that eight soldiers must accompany a constable who has to go into some sections of West Belfast.

RUC Chief Constable Hugh Annesley told the Helsinki Watch mission that roadblocks are essential to stop the movement of arms and ammunition, and are "a proper preventive policing method in Northern Ireland. If someone drives up at speed, and drives through a roadblock, it's a dilemma. When should you shoot? Should you jump out of the way? Is it all right if an IRA member is shot, but not a joyrider [rider in a stolen car]? There are no tidy answers."

Some others with whom the Helsinki Watch mission spoke share the government's view. John Alderdice, the leader of the Alliance Party, for example, said that, although he believes that some officers have sometimes shot with the purpose of killing, he does not believe there is a shoot to kill policy. He said he is gravely concerned about the Whiterock Road killings (discussed below), and believes there should be a formal investigation. He said that "if there is even one disputed killing, one must be concerned. But security force personnel are prime targets for murder, their whole lives. It's astonishing that more people haven't been killed."

A peace worker told us of following a young soldier walking down the street and hearing a torrent of verbal abuse directed at him. He told us that the armed forces suffer from stones thrown by children, insults from women and children, and constant fear of guns and bombs.

Fatal Shootings in 1990

During 1990, security forces in Northern Ireland killed ten people in six incidents; in four of these incidents, the circumstances were seriously disputed.

The Whiterock Road Case

In the first incident, on January 13, 1990, two plainclothes British soldiers shot and killed three men, Eddie Hale, Peter Thompson and John McNeill, who were robbing a betting shop on the Falls Road in West Belfast. According to the London *Independent* (January 16, 1990):

> The driver of the getaway car was shot first, with one soldier claiming he opened fire after the man made a suspicious movement. No gun or replica was found in the vehicle. It is not clear what warning, if any, the soldier gave before firing. There have been claims that this shooting was unjustifiable.
>
> When the other two would-be robbers emerged from the bookmaker's shop, both soldiers are believed to have opened fire on them . . . The official assessment is that it is most unlikely that a warning was given before the two hooded men were shot, but that it is unrealistic to expect that the soldiers should attempt to do so, given that they believed they were dealing with armed terrorists.
>
> Witnesses have claimed one soldier walked over to the two men as they lay on the ground and shot them again in the body or head. It is believed the soldier has told detectives he did fire at the men on the ground. He maintained, however, that they may have been moving and were potentially dangerous.

After the killings, the two soldiers quickly left the scene. It was later reported that one victim was carrying an imitation weapon and the other two were unarmed. They were shot a total of 28 times. The victims were petty thieves who had no connections with paramilitary

51

groups. Questions were raised as to why the men were not arrested rather than shot dead. Members of the British Parliament, political leaders and church officials called for an independent inquiry, but none took place.

Dr. Joe Hendron, an SDLP councillor, told the Helsinki Watch mission that he had arrived on the scene within half an hour. He said that the victims were "ordinary street hoods, not paramilitaries. They were not shot by young nervous 18-year-olds, but by the SAS. I can't accept that it was pure accident. These men had apparently been under surveillance for days ahead of the shootings."

In June 1990, Amnesty International raised these questions about the Whiterock Road killings:

* were the soldiers justified in opening fire without challenging the men?

* could the men have been arrested rather than killed?

* did the soldiers continue to shoot the robbers after they had been wounded and were clearly incapacitated?

* was the use of lethal force reasonable in the circumstances?

* were the killings part of a planned operation?

The case was investigated by the RUC (see procedure of investigations, below) and forwarded to the Director of Public Prosecutions (DPP).

On December 18, 1990, the DPP announced, without providing reasons, that the soldiers would not be prosecuted for the killings. Commenting on this decision, Dr. Hendron said: "How can I ask young people to support the police when the DPP has ruled that no one will be charged? At least if they were charged, the family would get some satisfaction. Young people laugh if you tell them to go to the police about something."

Two Teenage Joyriders

On September 30, British soldiers shot and killed two teenage joyriders, Karen Reilly and Martin Peake, in West Belfast. Police later issued a statement saying that soldiers had fired after the teenagers' car had driven through an army checkpoint, injuring one soldier. According to the Committee for the Administration Justice (CAJ), eyewitness accounts of the shooting significantly contradicted the police statement:

> Eugene Brannigan, whose car had been stopped by soldiers at the Glen Road near the junction of the Suffolk Road, said at a press conference that the teenagers' car had been traveling at speed around the junction and had swerved to avoid hitting the soldiers. The soldiers had been jittery, he said, and had earlier told him he would be shot if he tried anything. Brannigan also said he heard a policeman beside him say, "sure that car's been going about all day," implying that it was known that the car was being driven by unarmed joyriders.[45]

In July, six soldiers were charged in the incident: one was charged with murder, three with manslaughter, and all six with attempting to pervert the course of justice. The cases are pending.

Desmond Grew and Martin McCaughey

On October 9, 1990, two men, Desmond Grew and Martin McCaughey, died in a hail of gunfire near unused farm buildings in County Armagh in the south of Northern Ireland. The shootings were allegedly carried out by the SAS.[46] Questions were raised as to why the men were not captured rather than killed.

No charges have been brought against members of the security forces.

---

[45] *Just News*, Bulletin of Committee on the Administration of Justice, Vol. 5, No. 9, October 1990, page 1.

[46] *Ibid*.

Fergal Caraher

On December 30, 1990, Fergal Caraher, a 20-year-old married man and father of a one-year-old son, was shot and killed in his car by British Army troops at a checkpoint in his home village of Cullyhanna in South Armagh. Caraher was a member of Sinn Fein. His 23-year-old brother, Michael, was severely wounded in the same incident. According to the army account, the soldiers fired because Caraher's car had failed to stop at a checkpoint and had struck and injured two soldiers.

Eyewitnesses told a different story. Several people reported that the car drove off slowly a few minutes after having been waved through the checkpoint, that no soldiers were hit by the car, and that soldiers opened fire without warning and for no apparent reason.[47] The two soldiers who had allegedly been hit by Caraher's car were back on duty the day after the shootings.

Archbishop Cahal Daly, the leader of the Catholic Church in Ireland, along with other religious and political leaders, called for an independent investigation, but none has been initiated. No one has been charged with the killing.

Discussing the case with the Helsinki Watch mission, Father Raymond Murray, who has studied fatal shootings by security forces since 1969, said, "The security forces always say the victim broke through a checkpoint; no one believes it any more."[48]

---

[47]*The Irish Times*, January 5, 1991; *The Sunday Times*, (London) January 6, 1991; *The Independent*, January 7, 1991.

[48] In addition to the killings of the eight people described above, the CAJ reports that security forces killed two Irish National Liberation Army (INLA) members in 1990:
> * Martin Corrigan, an INLA operative, was killed in Armagh during an ambush on an RUC man's house in April 1990.
> * Alexander Patterson, an INLA operative, was shot by British undercover soldiers near Strabane, Co. Tyrone, on November 12, 1990. Official reports claimed an exchange of gunfire took place. Others were arrested after what appeared to be an attack on the home of a UDR man was foiled.

In June the local community convened an international inquiry into the case; its findings are to be issued in October 1991.

Standards for the Use of Lethal Force in Northern Ireland

The standard for the use of deadly force by security forces in Northern Ireland is set forth in Section 3(1) of the Criminal Law Act (NI) 1967: "A person may use such force *as is reasonable in the circumstances* in the prevention of crime, or in affecting or assisting in the lawful arrest of offenders or of persons unlawfully at large." [Emphasis added.]

In *Attorney General of Northern Ireland's Reference (No. 1 of 1975)*, the House of Lords stated:

Are we satisfied that no reasonable man

(a) with knowledge of such facts as were known to the accused or reasonably believed by him to exist

(b) in the circumstances and time available for reflection

(c) could be of the opinion that the prevention of the risk of harm to which others might be exposed if the suspect were allowed to escape, justified exposing the suspect to the risk of harm to him that might result from the kind of force that the accused contemplated using?[49]

The Committee on the Administration of Justice reports that the reasonableness standard has led prosecutors and judges to find most killings by security forces justifiable.[50]

In 1980 the British Army issued to its troops a "Yellow Card" with instructions on when to open fire in Northern Ireland. Based on an

---

[49] *Just News*, Bulletin of Committee on the Administration of Justice, Vol. 5, No. 2, February 1990, page 1.

[50] *Ibid*.

earlier version issued in 1972, the Yellow Card states: "firearms must only be used as a last resort . . . You may only open fire against a person if he is committing or about to commit an act *likely to endanger life and there is no other way to prevent the danger* [emphasis in original]." (See Appendix B for the full text of the Yellow Card.)

International Standards for the Use of Deadly Force

Article 6 of the International Covenant on Civil and Political Rights, which has been ratified by the UK, guarantees the right to life. The UN Human Rights Committee, which monitors the implementation of the Covenant, asserted in its general comment 6 (16) on Article 6:

> The deprivation of life by the authorities of the State is a matter of the utmost gravity. Therefore, the law must strictly control and limit the circumstances in which a person may be deprived of his life by such authorities.

Standards for the use of lethal force by security forces have been established in various international agreements and codes.

Article 2 of the European Convention for the Protection of Human Rights and Fundamental Freedoms (ECHR), to which the UK is a signatory, states:

> 1. Everyone's right to life shall be protected by law. No one shall be deprived of his life intentionally save in the execution of a sentence of a court following his conviction of a crime for which this penalty is provided by law.
>
> 2. Deprivation of life shall not be regarded as inflicted in contravention of this Article when it results from the use of force which is no more than *absolutely necessary*:
>
> > a) in defence of any person from unlawful violence;
> >
> > b) in order to effect a lawful arrest or to prevent the escape of a person lawfully detained;

56

c) in action lawfully taken for the purpose of quelling a riot or insurrection. [Emphasis added.]

Article 15 of the ECHR provides that there can be no derogation from Article 2 during time of war or public emergency, except for deaths resulting from lawful acts of war.

The International Covenant on Civil and Political Rights contains similar guarantees of the right to life (Article 6(l)) and also provides that there can be no derogation from that right "in time of public emergency which threatens the life of the nation" (Article 4).

The Code of Conduct for Law Enforcement Officials, adopted by the United Nations General Assembly on December 17, 1979, states in Article 3:

Law enforcement officials may use force only when *strictly necessary and to the extent required* for the performance of their duty. [Emphasis added.][51]

---

[51] The official Commentary to the Code states:
a) This provision emphasizes that the use of force by law enforcement officials should be exceptional; while it implies that law enforcement officials may be authorized to use force as is reasonably necessary under the circumstances for the prevention of crime or in effecting or assisting in the lawful arrest of offenders or suspected offenders, no force going beyond that may be used.
b) National law ordinarily restricts the use of force by law enforcement officials in accordance with a principle of *proportionality*. It is to be understood that such national principles of proportionality are to be respected in the interpretation of this provision. In no case should this provision be interpreted to authorise the use of force which is disproportionate to the legitimate objective to be achieved. [Emphasis added.]
c) The use of firearms is considered an extreme measure. Every effort should be made to exclude the use of firearms, especially against children. In general, firearms

In August 1990, the Eighth United Nations Congress on the Prevention of Crime and the Treatment of Offenders adopted "Basic Principles on the Use of Force and Firearms by Law Enforcement Officials," to be used for "the more effective implementation of the Code of Conduct for Law Enforcement Officials." Special Provision 9 of the Basic Principles states:

> Law enforcement officials shall not use firearms against persons except in self-defense or defense of others against the *imminent threat of death or serious injury,* to prevent the perpetration of a particularly serious crime involving grave threat to life, to arrest a person presenting such a danger and resisting their authority, or to prevent his or her escape, and only when less extreme means are insufficient to achieve these objectives. In any event, intentional lethal use of firearms may only be made when *strictly unavoidable* in order to protect life. [Emphasis added.]

The European Convention's requirement of *absolute necessity* for the use of lethal force, the Code of Conduct for Law Enforcement Officers' standard of strict necessity and the Basic Principles on the Use of Force and Firearms by Law Enforcement Officials' standard of strict unavoidability are all significantly stronger than the "reasonableness" standard found in the Northern Ireland Criminal Law Act.

* * *

---

should not be used except when a suspected offender offers armed resistance or otherwise jeopardizes the lives of others and less extreme measures are not sufficient to restrain or apprehend the suspected offender. In every instance in which a firearm is discharged, a report should be made promptly to the competent authorities.

The Helsinki Watch mission found that the "reasonableness" standard for the use of deadly force in Northern Ireland provides too much leeway for security forces to use lethal force and leads inevitably to abuses.

Helsinki Watch concludes that the standard for the use of deadly force should be one of "absolute necessity" as set forth in international standards and codes. In addition, the force used should be in proportion to the actual danger. The two key principles, therefore, are *absolute necessity* and *proportionality*. Helsinki Watch believes that it is incumbent on the government of the UK to enact legislation and to issue guidelines that will strictly control the use of lethal force in Northern Ireland.

Amnesty International has studied killings by security forces in Northern Ireland and has reached similar conclusions. Amnesty has stated that the law, as reflected in the standard that permits the use of force "as is reasonable in the circumstances," "is inadequate to prevent or deter the excessive use of lethal force by security forces."[52]

Amnesty International has urged the UK to "establish an independent judicial inquiry to review . . . the effectiveness of current legislation in providing clear guidance on the circumstances in which the use of lethal force is permissible and in deterring unlawful killings by members of the security forces."[53]

The Standing Advisory Commission on Human Rights, an advisory body whose members are appointed by the government, has recommended that the Criminal Law Act be amended to define the circumstances in which lethal force may be used. In October 1983, the Commission reported:

> [U]ncertainty about the rights and duties of the security
> forces in Northern Ireland may stem from the fact that
> not only are the security forces' instructions not public

---

[52] Amnesty International, *United Kingdom; Northern Ireland: Killings by Security Forces and "Supergrass Trials,"* EUR 45/08/88, June 1988, page 3.

[53] *Ibid.*, page 60.

knowledge but that the ordinary law has to be applied to circumstances with which it was not designed to cope. It must therefore be considered whether Section 3 of the Criminal Law Act (Northern Ireland) 1967 should be amended so as to define more precisely and comprehensively the circumstances in which it would be reasonable for the security forces to use potentially lethal force.

In March 1991, the SACHR issued a draft of a code of practice on the use of lethal force by security forces in Northern Ireland:

In all situations the minimum force necessary must be used. Firearms must only be used as a last resort. Where their use is unavoidable they must be used with restraint, in proportion to the seriousness of the offense and the legitimate objective to be achieved, and so as to minimise damage and injury and to respect and preserve human life.

The SACHR goes on to state that:

4. Firearms shall not be used against a person except in the following circumstances:

(1) in self-defence or defence of others against the imminent threat of death or serious injury;

(2) to prevent the commission of a particularly serious crime involving a grave threat to life;

(3) to effect the arrest of a person immediately presenting such a threat.

In all these cases firearms must not be used unless there is no other way to prevent the danger and it is strictly unavoidable to protect life.

See Appendix C for a complete copy of the SACHR's draft.

The Stevens Inquiry

In August 1989, allegations of collusion between British security forces and Loyalist paramilitaries became public when the Ulster Freedom Fighters (UFF), a Loyalist paramilitary group, claimed responsibility for the murder of Loughlin Maginn. The UFF claimed that official documents had been leaked to them that pointed to Maginn as a suspected IRA member. Over the next few months, the press reported that hundreds of photographs, files, personal information, information on house layouts and cars--all concerning members of the Nationalist community--had been leaked to Loyalist paramilitaries. Deputy Chief Constable John Stevens from Cambridgeshire in England was asked to conduct an independent inquiry.

In May 1990, the Stevens Inquiry issued a report concluding that:

* Information had been passed by security forces to paramilitary groups which had used it in attacks;

* Collusion in Northern Ireland is neither widespread nor institutionalized;

* Leakages of information from the security forces may never be completely eliminated;

* A Royal Ulster Constabulary anti-terrorist squad and serious crime unit should be set up;

* Higher standards of recruitment into the Ulster Defense Regiment are required; and

* Rigorous accounting and supervisory functions are needed to restrict production and availability of intelligence material.

Plastic Bullets

The plastic bullet is perhaps the most controversial weapon used by security forces in Northern Ireland; it has caused fourteen deaths and hundreds of injuries. Although it has been sharply criticized, the Royal Ulster Constabulary justifies use of the plastic bullet as a necessary means of crowd control that causes fewer and less severe injuries than live ammunition.

Plastic bullets are not used against paramilitaries; they are designed for use against rioters and have been in use in Northern Ireland for crowd control since 1973. Used first by the British Army, they were largely taken over by the RUC in 1978. According to the Northern Ireland Office, 55,367 plastic bullets were fired between 1973 and Dec. 31, 1990. The peak year was 1981, when 29,601 were fired. Since that time, use has declined markedly. Nine hundred thirty-seven plastic bullets were fired in 1989 and 257 in 1990.

The plastic bullet was introduced to replace the rubber bullet (which killed three people in 1972 and 1973) in the belief that plastic bullets are more effective, more accurate and not significantly more hazardous. The plastic bullet is nearly four inches long and 1.5 inches in diameter; its ends are flat. The bullet weighs 4.75 ounces. It leaves the barrel of a gun at a speed of 160 miles an hour.[54]

The Northern Ireland Office (NIO) says that "the riots which have taken place in Northern Ireland during the past 19 years differ from most of those which occur in other parts of Europe, having gone well beyond problems of crowd control."[55] It says that rioting in Northern Ireland can be extremely dangerous, necessitating a weapon which

---

[54] *Plastic Bullets and the Law*, Committee on the Administration of Justice Pamphlet No. 15, March 1990, page 1.

[55] "Riot Control and Baton Rounds in Northern Ireland," Northern Ireland Office, October 1989, page 1.

security forces can use to disperse rioters from a distance. "While small arms fire would often be justified (and is used in similar circumstances in other Western countries), it would cause more extensive injuries and greater loss of life."[56]

RUC Chief Constable Hugh Annesley told the Helsinki Watch mission that, to be accurate, plastic bullets must have a substantial charge, and that one needs to weigh the necessary weight and velocity against the potential to kill and injure. "Plastic bullets give you distance . . . When stones are thrown at security forces you need something to close the gap. With plastic bullets you can hold an area with a small number of men and limit casualties."

Since 1973, fourteen people have been killed by plastic bullets-- seven of them under the age of 16.[57] The most recent victim, Seamus Duffy, 15, was shot and killed on August 11, 1989, in Belfast. In addition to those killed, hundreds have been injured, many with life-changing injuries--blinded, brain-damaged, partially paralyzed, permanently disfigured.

Comparative figures regarding plastic and rubber bullets show that one person was killed for about every 18,000 rubber bullets fired, but that one person has been killed for about every 4,000 plastic bullets fired. This suggests that plastic bullets may be less accurate and/or more lethal than rubber bullets. As to the accuracy of the plastic bullet, Ian Hogg, the editor of *Jane's Counterinsurgency*, has stated:

> It's just a slab of plastic and with the best will in the world you can't guarantee where it's going to go when you pull the trigger--you do your best to aim at a specific spot but it has no ballistic shape, doesn't spin so it's not

---

[56] *Ibid.*

[57] For a complete list of deaths caused by rubber and plastic bullets, and the results of the coroners' inquests into those deaths, as compiled by the Committee on the Administration of Justice, see Appendix D.

stable that way, and it will hit and bounce and do all sorts of stupid things.[58]

The British Army's Rules of Engagement for plastic bullets, called "baton rounds," state:

General rules:

1. Baton rounds may be used to disperse a crowd whenever it is judged to be minimum and reasonable force in the circumstances.

2. The rounds must be fired at selected persons and not indiscriminately at the crowd. They should be aimed so that they strike the lower part of the target's body directly (i.e. without bouncing).

3. The authority to use these rounds is delegated to the commander on the spot.

Additional rules for the 25 grain PVC Baton Round:

4. Rounds must not be fired at a range of less than 20 meters except when the safety of soldiers or others is seriously threatened.

5. The baton round was designed and produced to disperse crowds. It can also be used to prevent an escape from HM Prisons if it is, in the circumstances, still considered to constitute the use of minimum and reasonable force. If a prisoner can be apprehended by hand, the baton must not be used.[59]

---

[58] Quoted in *Plastic Bullets and the Law*, Committee on the Administration of Justice Pamphlet No. 15, March 1990, page 40.

[59] *Ibid.*, page 7.

Analyzing the deaths and injuries caused by plastic bullets, the Committee on the Administration of Justice found that, although the bullets are not supposed to be aimed above the waist, most of the deaths and serious injuries were from bullets that struck the head or chest. This suggests that either the bullets are highly inaccurate, or that security forces are not following the Rules of Engagement and are aiming at upper bodies and heads.

As a result of coroners' inquests and civil law suits, it has been reported that only four of the fourteen people killed by plastic bullets had been involved in rioting. (See Appendix D.) This suggests that security forces are not following the Rules of Engagement; Rule 2 requires that rounds be fired at selected persons and not indiscriminately at a crowd.

Only one member of the security forces--a police officer--has been prosecuted in a plastic bullet case. In that case, Sean Downes was shot at an internment rally in 1984. Evidence produced during the manslaughter trial of an officer showed that the Rules of Engagement had not been followed: Downes had been hit in the chest and the bullet had been fired from less than twenty meters. The officer said in his defense that he had fired to protect two fellow officers whom he thought Downes was about to strike with a stick. Mr. Justice Hutton, now Lord Chief Justice, found him not guilty, and said:

> In the circumstances of sudden attacks I think it probable that the accused did act almost instinctively to defend his comrades without having time to assess the situation in the light of his knowledge of the police regulations.

Many civil suits for damages have been brought against the government for deaths or injuries suffered from plastic bullets. According to the CAJ, the Northern Ireland Office, the Police Authority and the Ministry of Defense have paid over a million pounds in compensation to victims of plastic bullets or their families in connection with these cases.[60]

---

[60] *Ibid.*, page 23.

Plastic bullets have not been used in England, Scotland or Wales, even on those occasions in which police officers have been attacked with stones and petrol bombs. Representatives of the British Home Office told the Helsinki Watch mission that plastic bullets are a tactic of last resort; some officers have been trained to use them, but police have not found it necessary to do so. Police manage with truncheons, shields and, in rare cases, tear gas. The Home Office representatives said that a decision to use plastic bullets would be made only at the highest levels of the police force.

The Catholic Bishops of Northern Ireland have called the use of plastic bullets "morally indefensible," and the European Parliament has twice called for them to be banned.[61]

The Helsinki Watch mission met in January with members of the United Campaign Against Plastic Bullets, including victims and relatives of victims. The mission talked with Brendan Duffy, the father of Seamus Duffy, a 15-year-old who was killed with a plastic bullet in August 1989. The RUC claimed that Seamus Duffy had been involved in rioting. At a four-day coroner's inquest in June 1990, a jury found evidence that Duffy had been rioting earlier, but no evidence that he had been rioting just before he was shot. The jury also accepted a state pathologist's finding that the boy had been shot from a distance of about ten yards.[62] After an internal investigation supervised by the Independent Commission for Police Complaints, the Director of Public Prosecutions decided that no prosecutions would be brought against RUC members.[63]

Brendan Duffy told the mission that Seamus had been shot in the heart with a plastic bullet with its aluminum cap still on (the cap is

---

[61] Press release, July 4, 1983, and press releases on December 14, 1981 and October 11, 1984. Cited in *Justice Under Fire: The Abuse of Civil Liberties in Northern Ireland*. Anthony Jennings, Ed. Pluto Press, London, 1990. Page 142.

[62] *Just News*, Committee on the Administration of Justice, Vol. 5, No. 7, July/August 1990. Page 1.

[63] Communication from the Committee on the Administration of Justice, March 11, 1991.

supposed to drop off as the bullet is fired). Mr. Duffy said that the RUC treated the family abusively at the hospital where Seamus was taken; when Mrs. Duffy argued with an RUC constable, she was shoved roughly, and another constable put a gun to Mr. Duffy's head and asked him, "Do you want to be next?"

According to the British Information Service:

> Plastic baton rounds would never be used if demonstrations, processions and meetings were held in an orderly manner, within the law. Their use in Northern Ireland has declined dramatically over recent years; however, when rioting and attacks on policemen and soldiers put life or property seriously at risk, they are sometimes the only effective way of restoring order, saving lives and avoiding injuries. The security forces keep their riot control methods under continual review and monitor all developments, at home and abroad, that might enable them to cope better with public disorder while adhering to the principle of minimum force. So far, however, a safer yet equally effective alternative to plastic baton rounds has not been found.[64]

* * *

Helsinki Watch believes that the use of plastic bullets in Northern Ireland should be banned immediately. The Helsinki Watch mission found that plastic bullets have been lethal in 14 instances, and in hundreds of others have injured people--some gravely. It may be that the bullets are inherently unstable and inaccurate; it may be that the regulations on their use are inadequate; it may be that insufficient controls have been exercised over the use of such weapons; it may be that all of these conjectures are true. For whatever reason, it is clear that plastic bullets kill.

---

[64] Leaflet, "Human Rights in Northern Ireland," given to Helsinki Watch in December 1990.

It is also true that members of security forces need some sort of intermediate weapon--something between a truncheon and live ammunition--to protect themselves in riot situations. In Helsinki Watch's opinion, the plastic bullet is not such an instrument, and, judging from its declining use, the authorities are increasingly sensitive to this fact. We believe that the burden is on the UK and the Northern Ireland Office to find an alternative intermediate weapon the use of which does not violate human rights standards.

IV. INVESTIGATION OF THE USE OF LETHAL FORCE BY SECURITY FORCES

For many years observers have raised questions about the investigation of the use of lethal force by security forces in Northern Ireland--about the small proportion of security force members prosecuted for killings, about the methods of investigation into charges, about the available charges themselves, and about the Coroners' Inquests.

Security Force Members and Disputed Killings

Members of the security forces in Northern Ireland killed 329 people between 1969 and 1989; 178 (54 percent) were civilians with no known connections to paramilitary groups.[65] The circumstances of many of these killings have been disputed. Killings by security forces did not end in 1989. Appendix E contains a list of 48 incidents in which 73 people met their deaths at the hands of security forces between 1982 and 1991, and briefly details the circumstances in which they were killed.[66] Since 1969, prosecutions have been brought in nineteen cases against security force members who killed people while on duty. (See Appendix F for a list of 17 prosecutions; the prosecution of four UDR men for the murder of Adrian Carroll is the eighteenth, and the prosecution of six soldiers for the killing of two teenage joyriders, Karen Reilly and Martin Peake, (see Chapter III) is the nineteenth.)

In only three cases have defendants been found guilty of murder or manslaughter. In the first, defendant Davidson was found guilty in 1981 of manslaughter in the death of Theresa Donaghy and sentenced to 12 months' detention in Young Offenders' Centre.[67]

---

[65] See Table III in Chapter III.

[66] Six incidents involving the killing of ten people in 1990 were described in detail in Chapter III.

[67] *Justice Under Fire: The Abuse of Civil Liberties in Northern Ireland.* Anthony Jennings, ed. London: Pluto Press, 1990. Page 105.

In the second, a notorious case which was cited repeatedly to the Helsinki Watch mission, Private Ian Thain was found guilty of the murder of Thomas Reilly in 1984. He is the only member of the regular British Army to have been found guilty of a murder committed in Northern Ireland while on duty.[68] Thomas Reilly was involved in an altercation with an army foot patrol in August 1983. According to testimony presented at the trial, a corporal told Private Thain to "get" Reilly as he ran away, naked above the waist. Thain ran after Reilly, shouting "stop or I'll shoot." Thain said that he shot Reilly after Reilly turned back slightly toward him and his hand could no longer be seen. Thain's testimony that he believed Reilly was reaching for a gun was not believed by the trial judge. The Court of Appeal upheld the verdict.

Private Thain served only two years and three months of his life sentence and was allowed to rejoin his regiment, although not to return to Northern Ireland.[69] His case was cited to show that only one regular British Army soldier had ever been convicted of murder while on duty in Northern Ireland, and that even he was imprisoned for a very short portion of his sentence.

The small number of prosecutions of police and military, and the DPP's failure to recommend such prosecutions (as in the Whiterock Road case discussed earlier), have led a sizeable portion of the Nationalist community in Northern Ireland to believe that serious efforts are rarely

---

[68] In one case, security force members were convicted of a killing committed when off duty. On April 8, 1985, Martin Love was shot and killed in Enniskillen as he returned home from a local hotel. A UDR man and a British soldier were convicted of his killing and sentenced to life; both had been off duty at the time of the shooting. Committee for the Administration of Justice, communications March 11 and March 21, 1991.

In an earlier case, Adrian Carroll was shot dead in Armagh city on November 8, 1983. Four members of the UDR were convicted and given life sentences in July 1986. According to the Crown's case, the soldiers were on patrol. In January 1991 a dossier with new evidence on the case, known as the case of the "UDR 4," was presented to Secretary of State Peter Brooke in an effort to convince the authorities that there has been a miscarriage of justice. CAJ communications March 11 and 21, 1991.

[69] *Ibid.*, pages 121 and 122.

made to investigate killings by the police and the military. It has led, we were told, to a lack of confidence in the security forces and in the government to which they are accountable.[70]

The Helsinki Watch mission was told that it is very difficult to convict members of the security forces of murder. "There is a protective shield around the security forces," said Alex Attwood of the SDLP. "The government will not let justice take its course," said Father Raymond Murray of Armagh.

The Government's View

The UK asserts that all disputed killings are thoroughly investigated and that, where indicated, responsible security force members are prosecuted. In a leaflet entitled, "Human Rights in Northern Ireland," given to the Helsinki Watch mission in December 1990 by the British Information Service, the government states:

---

[70] Public confidence in police investigations of killings by police officers was profoundly shaken by the Stalker inquiry in 1984. John Stalker, Deputy Chief Constable of Greater Manchester, England, was asked to go to Northern Ireland to investigate killings by security forces of six unarmed men in three separate incidents in a five-week period in 1982. All had been killed by members of a special RUC anti-terrorist unit. Stalker was also asked to investigate the RUC's investigation of the three incidents. Northern Ireland police reacted to his efforts with hostility and obstructionist tactics. Before he could complete his task, Stalker was removed from the case and charged with disciplinary offenses unrelated to the inquiry; the charges were subsequently dropped. Stalker's investigation was completed by another officer, but the findings were never released. Stalker later wrote a book, *The Stalker Affair*. He concluded that the RUC's investigation into the killings had been uncoordinated, inept and improper; rules for the preservation of evidence had been blatantly ignored; detectives had been denied access to the police officers who had killed the six and to forensic examinations of their car, clothes, hands and weapons. As for the killings themselves, he concluded that "each left a strong suspicion that a type of pre-planned police ambush had occurred, and that someone had led these men to their deaths" (page 72).

Like everyone else, the security forces must obey the law and are answerable to the courts for their actions. Every incident involving the army or police that results in death or serious injury is fully and impartially investigated; and on the direction of the DPP [Director of Public Prosecutions] (Northern Ireland) a number of individual members of the security forces have been charged and convicted of murder in such incidents.

Some police officers believe that police are brought up on disciplinary charges too often. Drew Nelson, a lawyer and an Ulster Unionist Party candidate for South Down, told the Helsinki Watch mission that he has many clients who are police officers; he stated:

The police on the ground feel they are hard done by the structure of discipline. For the last five years, there has been a lack of morale, a feeling that police are more easily sacrificed by superiors. Police in the lower ranks feel that Catholics in the police force can get away with anything; they are encouraged and promoted.

The Investigation Process

Thousands of complaints are lodged each year against the security forces operating in Northern Ireland. According to the RUC Chief Constable's Annual Report for 1989, 2,484 cases involving 3,989 complaints against police were received during that year. Of those, 2,404 complaints were "withdrawn or not proceeded with," 1,326 were not substantiated, 58 were substantiated, and 201 were "informally resolved." Of the 609 complaints alleging assault that were investigated, only 16 (2.6 percent) were substantiated; another 24 were informally resolved. Only five (2.4 percent) of the 204 complaints of oppressive conduct or harassment were substantiated; another 41 were informally resolved. The Helsinki Watch mission was unable to obtain statistics on the number of complaints filed against the Army during that time.

Investigations into complaints against security forces are handled as follows:

Complaints that allege misconduct not of a criminal nature are handled by the individual service--the army informally investigates complaints against soldiers and the RUC investigates complaints against the police.

Complaints that allege criminal conduct, whether against police, army or UDR, are investigated by a special unit within the RUC. Investigations into allegations of criminal conduct by the police are supervised by the Independent Commission for Police Complaints for Northern Ireland (ICPC), an organization that was set up by the Police (Northern Ireland) Order 1987, following the uproar caused by, among other things, the Stalker inquiry.

The ICPC is required to supervise any investigation in which there has been a death or serious injury; it may supervise other complaints if it believes doing so is in the public interest. The ICPC has no subpoena power, or other power to investigate on its own, or to initiate investigations; it can only supervise police investigations.

Brian Reid, the only full-time ICPC member, told us that supervision consists of approving (or disapproving) of the investigating officer assigned to the case; meeting with him or her to discuss the investigation; sitting in on interviews with complainants, witnesses and police officers, if advisable, and if time permits; and deciding with the investigating officer whether the investigation is complete. At the end of the investigation, the member issues a letter stating whether the investigation was satisfactory. So far, he told us, the ICPC has not issued a letter describing an investigation as unsatisfactory.

A report is then sent to the Director of Public Prosecution (DPP), who decides whether or not to prosecute. If he decides to prosecute, the case goes to court. According to the Chief Constable's 1989 Annual Report, 1,314 cases (out of the total of 2,484) were referred to the DPP during that year, but the DPP directed prosecutions in only eight cases involving eleven officers.

If the DPP decides against prosecution, the case is returned to the Deputy Chief Constable (DCC) of the RUC, who decides whether there

73

has been a breach of the RUC Disciplinary Code. If the DCC decides not to take disciplinary action, the ICPC has the power to direct him to take such action. According to Mr. Reid, the ICPC normally agrees with the DCC.

The ICPC reports that in 1990 it supervised 888 cases with a total of 1680 allegations. Of the 1680 allegations, 688 (40.9 percent) were of assaults. Of the 888 cases, 785 were referred to the Director of Public Prosecutions. At the end of 1990, the DPP had directed criminal charges to be brought in only sixteen (2 percent) of these referrals.[71]

If a police officer is charged with a crime, the RUC can bring disciplinary proceedings once the criminal case has ended. The RUC's Discipline Code lists 18 offenses for which a police officer may be charged, ranging from misconduct and neglect of duty to criminal conduct.

If a police officer is convicted of a crime, s/he may be charged with the disciplinary offense of "criminal conduct" and punished by dismissal, requirement to resign, reduction in rank, reduction in salary (for up to 12 months), fine, reprimand and caution.

If a police officer is acquitted of a criminal charge, s/he may not be charged with a disciplinary offense that is substantially the same as the crime that was charged. The standard of proof used in disciplinary hearings is "beyond a reasonable doubt," the same standard that is used in a criminal trial. The Helsinki Watch mission was told by lawyers and others in Northern Ireland that this high standard of proof is one of the factors that diminishes the efficacy of disciplinary proceedings.

The ICPC has no authority to supervise an RUC investigation of the army or the UDR. Further, there is no independent body that either supervises or examines the army's investigations of complaints against its troops. In February 1991, Northern Ireland Minister of State Brian Mawhinney announced that an independent lay commissioner would be appointed. This is provided for in Section 60 of the 1991 EPA.

---

[71] *Third Annual Report, 1990*, Independent Commission for Police Complaints for Northern Ireland, 1991. Page 17.

During 1989, the army received 282 formal non-criminal complaints against its members. The army reported that 41 percent of these were "denied"; 36 percent "not substantiated;" 9 percent substantiated; and 2 percent "fault on both sides." Another 12 percent were outstanding at the end of the year.[72]

Although thousands of complaints are filed each year against police officers and soldiers, many more people apparently do not file complaints. In his 1990 review of the EPA, Lord Colville reported that

> Effective complaints procedures are essential especially while emergency laws are in force; although the police and Army make considerable efforts to deal with complaints swiftly and effectively, there is a widespread feeling that very few complaints are satisfactorily resolved, especially in terms of the receipt of an apology.[73]

> There is certainly an impression retained by some that there is no point in complaining, in that no confidence can be placed on the procedures; or worse that complainants may anticipate harassment by way of reprisal. Levels of complaints from West Belfast and West Londonderry, which contain about half of the Catholic community in NI, are low. It is disconcerting to meet people, such as priests, who have cultivated good relationships with senior officers of the Army and police operating in their areas, but still say they have almost never had a complaint resolved satisfactorily, in the sense

---

[72] *Review of the Northern Ireland (Emergency Provisions) Acts, 1978 and 1987.* Viscount Colville of Culross QC. London: HMSO, July 1990. (Colville report) Page 20.

[73] *Ibid.*, p. 66.

of receiving an apology for misbehaviour. I have no doubt that this is not just a received attitude, so much as a reflection of recent experience.[74]

Helsinki Watch recommends that the Independent Commission for Police Complaints take an increasingly active and independent role in the investigative process.

International Agreements on the Effective Investigation of Killings by Security Forces

On May 24, 1989, the UN Economic and Social Council, on the recommendation of the Committee on Crime Prevention and Control, adopted "Principles on the Effective Prevention and Investigation of Extra-Legal, Arbitrary and Summary Executions." (The full texts of the sections on investigation and legal proceedings are reprinted in Appendix G.)

These principles set forth a thorough and detailed agenda for the investigation of killings by security forces and subsequent legal proceedings, including requirements for:

* a thorough, prompt and impartial investigation of all suspected cases of extra-legal, arbitrary and summary executions;

* power in the investigative authority to obtain all information necessary to the inquiry; authority to oblige witnesses and officials allegedly involved in any such executions to appear and testify, and to demand the production of evidence;

* an independent commission of inquiry for those cases in which the established investigative procedures are inadequate because of lack of expertise or impartiality, and for cases where there are complaints from the family

---

[74] *Ibid.*, p. 21.

of the victim about these inadequacies or other substantial reasons;

* an adequate autopsy conducted by an impartial and independent physician who is an expert in forensic pathology and is given access to all investigative data;

* protection from violence or intimidation for complainants, witnesses, families and investigators;

* removal from power or control over complainants, witnesses, families or investigators of anyone potentially implicated in extra-legal, summary or arbitrary executions;

* access by families and their legal representatives to any hearing and to all relevant information, and the right to present other evidence;

* right of a family to have a representative present at the autopsy;

* a detailed written report on the methods and findings of the investigation to be made public within a reasonable time;

* a government response to the report of the investigation within a reasonable time, either replying to the report or indicating the steps to be taken in response to it;

* government action to bring to justice persons identified by the investigation as having taken part in extra-legal, arbitrary and summary executions;

* no right to claim an order from a superior officer or a public authority as justification for extra-legal, summary or arbitrary execution;

* responsibility of superiors, officers or other public officials for acts committed under their authority if they had a reasonable opportunity to prevent such acts; no blanket immunity from prosecution to any person involved in such acts; and

* fair and adequate compensation for the families and dependents of victims of extra-legal, arbitrary and summary executions within a reasonable period of time.

* * *

The Helsinki Watch mission found that investigations of disputed killings by security forces in Northern Ireland have not met the standards set forth in the UN Principles on the Effective Prevention and Investigation of Extra-Legal, Arbitrary and Summary Executions. The infrequency of prosecution of members of security forces who have, in some cases, shot and killed unarmed persons, the fact that the RUC itself investigates killings by the RUC, the secrecy surrounding investigations and the DPP's decision as to whether to prosecute, the failure to prosecute not only the security force member responsible but also superior officers who may have ordered such acts--all of these factors suggest inadequate investigations that are neither impartial nor independent.

Helsinki Watch recommends that the United Kingdom abide by the UN Principles and carry out thorough, prompt and impartial investigations of all suspected cases of extra-legal, arbitrary or summary executions.

Amnesty International has urged the government of the UK to "establish an independent judicial inquiry to review all the disputed incidents of killings since 1982, with a view to considering the procedures used to bring out the full facts in such incidents. The inquiry should also investigate the allegations that external inquiry was obstructed."[75] Helsinki Watch supports this recommendation as well.

---

[75] Amnesty International, *Killings by Security Forces and "Supergrass Trials," op. cit.*, page 60.

Limitations on Charges Against Security Officers

A serious problem in the prosecution of security force members for fatal shootings is that, once a police officer or soldier intentionally kills someone, he or she may be charged only with the offense of murder --no lesser charge, such as manslaughter or intentionally causing grievous bodily harm-- can be filed.[76] The Helsinki Watch mission was told by lawyers and human rights activists that the lack of a lesser charge was a significant factor in the DPP's decision as to whether to prosecute a police officer or soldier.

The rule that only a charge of murder may be brought in a killing by security forces was upheld by the House of Lords in *The Attorney General for Northern Ireland's Reference (No. 1 of 1975)*. In that case a soldier, Lance Corporal Jones, was acquitted of the murder of farmhand Patrick McElhone. When Jones approached McElhone on his farm to question him, McElhone ran away; the soldier shot and killed him. McElhone was unarmed and it was admitted at trial that he was not involved in any way with terrorist activity.

Corporal Jones testified that when he fired he honestly believed that McElhone was a member of the Provisional IRA who was trying to escape, and that he had no other way to stop him. The Court of Appeal and the House of Lords ruled that if a defendant had the necessary intent the offense was murder, which carries a mandatory life sentence. Corporal Jones had intended to shoot McElhone; he had therefore to be charged with murder, and not with a lesser offense.

The requirement that murder must be charged in a fatal shooting by a security force member is a major barrier to prosecuting and convicting police and military: the RUC does not want to recommend murder charges, DPPs do not want to charge police and military with murder, and courts do not want to convict them of murder.

---

[76] The charge of manslaughter is still available for cases in which a shooting was accidental--when a security force member discharges a gun by mistake, or with no intention of shooting at someone. This was apparently the case in *R. v. Davidson*, cited earlier in this section, in which defendant Davidson was found guilty of manslaughter in the death of Theresa Donaghy in 1981.

The Helsinki Watch mission concluded that the lack of a lesser charge than murder in fatal shootings by members of security forces in Northern Ireland has adversely affected the criminal justice system's ability to deal appropriately with such killings. Helsinki Watch believes that a lesser offense of manslaughter should be incorporated into the Criminal Code applicable to Northern Ireland for those situations in which excessive force is used in self-defense or to prevent crime. Other lesser offenses, such as "breach of police or army regulations," or "unlawful use of a firearm," or "unreasonable or excessive use of force," would also be useful.

The Helsinki Watch recommendations are supported by others. The Standing Advisory Commission on Human Rights and the Committee on the Administration of Justice have both recommended that a lesser offense should be available in fatal shootings by security forces. In January 1991, the SACHR stated:

> The overall objective in the opinion of the Commission should be to provide a range of possible charges of varying gravity which might be laid in cases where lethal force is unjustifiably used. In cases where there has merely been a reprehensible error of judgement a charge of the breach of the code would be appropriate; in cases where there has been a reckless disregard of life or a gross violation of the code a charge of manslaughter might be appropriate; and in cases where there is evidence of a preconceived plan to use lethal force rather than to effect an arrest in a planned ambush or confrontation a charge of murder might be appropriate. Provision for a range of possible charges of this kind would go a long way to remove the feeling in some sections of the community that members of the security forces cannot in practice be made personally liable for unlawful conduct in cases of this kind.

Lord Colville, in his Report on the Operation in 1988-89 of the Northern Ireland (Emergency Provisions) Acts 1978 and 1987, suggested in his section on Excessive Use of Force in Murder Cases that a middle course was needed between finding a soldier or police officer guilty of murder and full acquittal (Para. 8.5.6).

In 1989, the House of Lords' Select Committee on Murder and Life Imprisonment recommended the creation of a new defense reducing murder to manslaughter where excessive force was used:

> Where a person kills in a situation in which it is reasonable for some force to be used in self-defense or in the prevention of crime but the defendant used excessive force . . . if, at the time of the act, he honestly believed that the force he used was reasonable in the circumstances.

Coroners' Inquests

Because there are so few prosecutions for fatal shootings by security forces, a coroner's inquest is often the only proceeding at which a victim's family, the press and the public can get information about a killing. Inquests thus take on considerable importance.

Coroners are appointed by the Lord Chancellor; they must be lawyers with at least five years' experience practicing law. An inquest is initiated in circumstances of unexplained, unexpected or suspicious deaths pursuant to the Coroners Act (Northern Ireland) 1959. In a death that is not due to natural causes, a coroner may hold an inquest, but is not legally required to do so. An inquest must be held in cases in which a death occurred in prison or "in circumstances the continuance or possible recurrence of which is prejudicial to the health or safety of the public or any section of the public."[77]

A coroner's inquest is not a trial; according to the Northern Ireland Court Service, it is

> an inquiry which is held into the circumstances and the medical cause of a death and to establish the facts. The

---

[77] Coroners Act (Northern Ireland) 1959, Section 18.

purpose of the inquest is to ascertain the identity of the deceased, when, where and how the death occurred, and to establish the particulars which have to be registered by the Registrar of Deaths. The inquest does not attempt to allocate responsibility for the death, as a trial would do. It is held in public, sometimes with a jury. It is for the Coroner to organise the inquest in a way to best serve the public interest and the interest of the relatives.[78]

A jury is made up of between seven and eleven people; the jury, not the coroner, formulates findings. The coroner decides which witnesses to call. "Properly interested persons," including lawyers, family members or others, may question witnesses. Inquests are public.

Where a charge of murder, manslaughter or certain other offenses is made, the inquest is adjourned until the criminal proceedings have been concluded. At the end of the criminal proceedings, the coroner may, but is not required to resume the inquest.

The Helsinki Watch mission heard many complaints about inquests from lawyers and the families of victims. First, extensive delays result from the practice that an inquest be adjourned until the completion of criminal proceedings.[79] In England and Wales, inquests are not adjourned indefinitely, but for a specified period of time; if at the end of that period authorities have not reached a decision on whether to prosecute, the coroner's inquest proceeds.

Second, coroners' juries in Northern Ireland have limited powers; they are not permitted to reach full verdicts such as "unlawful killing by unnamed persons." Only factual findings, such as "death resulted from a bullet in the head," can be made. The jury may not express a view on the lawfulness of a killing. Coroners' juries in England and Wales are

---

[78] "The Work of the Coroner in Northern Ireland: Some Questions Answered." A Northern Ireland Court Service Guide, January 1989. Page 4.

[79] Delays can last for years while decisions are reviewed in the courts; an inquest into the November 1982 deaths of Gervaise McKerr, Eugene Toman and Sean Burns is still pending.

permitted to make findings of "unlawful killings" in cases of murder, manslaughter or infanticide.[80]

Third, anyone who is suspected of causing a death or who may be charged with an offense related to it is not required to testify at the inquest, but may submit written testimony.[81] This means, of course, that such testimony is not subject to cross-examination, a procedure upheld by the House of Lords in *In Re McK (Northern Ireland)* (1990). In England, a person suspected of causing a death, including a police officer or soldier, may be compelled to appear at an inquest, but is not obliged to answer a question that might be incriminating.

Legal assistance is not available to indigent families of victims of shootings by security forces. Moreover, families and their representatives do not have access before an inquest to evidence, such as autopsy reports, witnesses' statements and other evidence, making cross-examination quite difficult.

Helsinki Watch recommends that the Coroners Law and Rules in Northern Ireland should, at a minimum, be changed to bring them into line with the law in England and Wales:

> * In cases in which criminal charges may be brought against a suspect, the coroner's inquest should be adjourned for a specific period of time; if at the end of that time the DPP has not decided whether to prosecute, the inquest should be resumed;

> * Coroners' juries should have the power to reach a full verdict, such as "unlawful killing by unnamed persons;"

---

[80] Form 18 for verdicts, as amended under the Coroners (Amendment) Rules 1977. Cited in Committee on the Administration of Justice 1983 memo on "Coroners' Inquests on Disputed Killings in Northern Ireland."

[81] The question of whether these written statements should be admissible is currently waiting to be heard before the House of Lords on a judicial review appeal.

* Persons who are suspected of causing the death at issue should be compelled to testify in person but should not be required to answer questions that might incriminate themselves;

* Families of victims killed by security forces should be eligible for legal aid assistance so that they can be aided before and during the inquest by an attorney; and

* Families of victims should have access to autopsy reports, documents, witnesses' statements and other evidence to be introduced at an inquest, and adequate time to prepare for the inquest after receiving this information.

V. THE RIGHT TO A FAIR TRIAL

For many years, questions have been raised by a wide range of observers as to whether suspects in Northern Ireland accused of acts of political violence or related offenses receive fair trials. These questions concern aspects of the Diplock Courts (special courts set up under the Northern Ireland (Emergency Provisions) Act) including the requirement for non-jury trials, the nature of the offenses that are tried in Diplock courts, the standard for admitting confessions into evidence, the right of a suspect to remain silent without prejudice,[82] and threats to lawyers.

The Diplock Courts

In 1972, shortly after the British government imposed direct rule in Northern Ireland, a commission chaired by Lord Diplock made recommendations "to deal more effectively with terrorism without using internment."[83] In December 1972, the Commission recommended a series of steps that were subsequently enacted by Parliament as the Northern Ireland (Emergency Provisions) Act 1973 (since amended in 1978, 1987 and 1991).

One of the major recommendations of the Diplock Commission was that jury trial in Northern Ireland should be suspended for the duration of the emergency for serious offenses (referred to as "scheduled offenses") that were thought to be related to the unrest. The Commission

---

[82] The standard for admitting confessions into evidence and the right of a suspect to remain silent without prejudice are discussed in Chapter II.

[83] Secretary of State for Northern Ireland William Whitelaw, M.P., House of Commons Debates (*Hansard*), April 17, 1973, col. 276. The Unionist government in Northern Ireland had introduced internment without trial in August 1971 under the Civil Authorities (Special Powers) Act 1922. This act had been met with intense domestic and international criticism and a sharp increase in violence in Northern Ireland.

reported that jury trial was "not practicable in the case of terrorist crimes in Northern Ireland"[84] in light of:

* the threat of intimidation of witnesses and jurors; and

* the possibility of "perverse verdicts," that is, verdicts based on political or sectarian grounds, rather than on the evidence adduced during the trial of a case.

The Commission believed that Unionist defendants were being "perversely acquitted" by predominantly Loyalist juries, and that the possibility existed for "perverse convictions" of Republican paramilitaries by Unionist juries as well. The Commission concluded (without systematic investigation into the nature of the problem) that jurors would be intimidated by both Loyalist and Republican paramilitary groups.

A schedule of twenty-one offenses was appended to the Northern Ireland (Emergency Provisions) Act (EPA) 1973, including murder, manslaughter, rioting, kidnapping, assault resulting in bodily harm, robbery, use of explosives and petrol bombs, and arson.[85] There is no requirement in the EPA that a scheduled offense be associated with political violence.

Thousands of cases involving serious offenses have been tried in these non-jury "Diplock" courts. In the rest of the United Kingdom, serious criminal cases are tried before juries, even when political violence is a factor.

Not all of the serious offense cases in Northern Ireland have been tried in Diplock courts. The EPA gives the Attorney General the authority to certify that particular cases of murder, manslaughter and offenses against the person should not be treated as scheduled offenses

---

[84] *Report of the Commission to Consider Legal Procedures to Deal with Terrorist Activities in Northern Ireland,* Lord Diplock, Chairman. London, HMSO, December 1972 (The Diplock Report). Chapter 5, Para. 36.

[85] See Appendix H for the Schedule of Offenses.

and therefore should be tried by juries. This process has become known as "scheduling out." The cases that are scheduled out are those in which political violence is not thought to have been a factor. Between 1982 and 1986, the Attorney General received 2,685 applications for decertification of scheduled offenses; he approved 1,865--69.5 percent. The Attorney General's decision not to schedule out a case is not subject to appellate review. The exact number of cases in which defendants have been tried in Diplock courts for crimes that were not associated with political violence is not known, although it was estimated in 1984 that 40 percent of the Diplock cases involved offenses unrelated to political violence.[86]

A major issue in the criminal justice system in Northern Ireland is whether Diplock courts should be abandoned and jury trials reinstituted for all or some criminal offenses now tried before a judge alone.

Jury trials are not required by international law. On the other hand, the International Covenant on Civil and Political Rights provides, in Article 14, that "All persons shall be equal before the courts and the tribunals." At the present time, those being tried before Diplock courts are not being treated "equally" whether the comparison is made to trials of other persons accused of crime in Northern Ireland (non-scheduled offenses) or to trials of persons accused of identical offenses in other parts of the United Kingdom. These significant inequalities raise a presumption that Diplock courts are in violation of human rights standards.

This presumption is strengthened when one recognizes that trial by jury has been one of the central elements of the British system of justice for hundreds of years--"a cherished and vital component of the legal tradition of Britain and Ireland for centuries."[87] This long

---

[86] D. Walsh, *Civil Liberties in Northern Ireland*. National Council on Civil Liberties Review of 1984. Page 326. Cited in Hellerstein, McKay and Schlam, *Criminal Justice and Human Rights in Northern Ireland*, Committee on International Human Rights of the Association of the Bar of the City of New York, 1987, page 67.

[87] S. C. Greer and A. White, *Abolishing the Diplock Courts*. London: The Cobden Trust, 1986. Page 78.

tradition is buttressed by strong policy reasons that support jury trials as the preferred mode of resolving criminal cases:

> * Determination of guilt or innocence by a representative portion of the community is the most reliable fact-finding mechanism;

> * Having ordinary men and women take part in the criminal justice process increases public confidence in the system;

> * Jury trials involve fresh tribunals for each case, and the system therefore avoids the "case-hardening" that takes place when judges hear similar cases repetitively;

> * A judge who rules a confession inadmissible because of torture or ill-treatment may not be able to ignore the confession in trying the case; if the case is heard by a jury and a judge rules a confession inadmissible, the jury will not know about the confession and thus will not be influenced by it; and

> * Serving on a jury is an important right and obligation in a democratic system.[88]

For these reasons of history and principle it is appropriate to place a burden of persuasion on the authorities who justify the use of non-jury Diplock courts. Before suspending a crucial right, even during an emergency and for a select list of offenses, great care must be taken

---

[88] The fundamental importance of jury trial to criminal justice was recently expressed by the Supreme Court of New Jersey in an opinion by Justice Daniel O'Hern in the case of *State v. Dixon*:

> But there is an enduring value to the principle that only juries can decide our guilt or innocence. If people had to choose the liberties they would give up, we think the right to have a jury determine their guilt would be among the last surrendered. It is that right we are enforcing.

The New York Times, August 4, 1991, p. 16.

to be sure that such drastic action is truly necessary. Helsinki Watch does not believe that this burden has been met for the system as it currently operates in Northern Ireland.

In reaching this conclusion, we are mindful of the exceptional conditions that confront law enforcement officials in the Province. The long history of communal strife and the appalling statistics of killings, maimings and bombings both testify to the special if not unique circumstances in which the police and courts must function. Such sobering facts raise a permissible inference that normal law enforcement rules need not be followed. But they do not adequately justify the current arrangement, as we now explain.

Initially, it is important to recognize that there is substantial opinion that the decision to abolish juries in scheduled cases was not based on sufficient study or evidence.

In 1986, S. C. Greer and A. White, writing in *Abolishing the Diplock Courts*, said:

> An examination of the Diplock report and the parliamentary debates in 1973 shows that the evidence presented to justify the introduction of non-jury courts was seriously deficient and at most indicated that eligibility for jury service should have been democratised, the selection of juries randomised and the identity of jurors concealed. Ironically, in 1974 the first two of these principles were introduced to those parts of the jury system left unaffected by the EPA but the implications of these changes for the Diplock system were never adequately considered by Parliament.
>
> . . . We do not claim that there was no intimidation of jurors in the early 1970s nor that perverse acquittals was not a problem. We maintain merely that it was never shown that these were such serious defects that the suspension of trial by jury rather than some less radical alternative was required. It is our conclusion, therefore, that the case for the Diplock courts was orginally, and remains astonishingly weak and that jury trial for

scheduled offences should, therefore, be re-introduced forthwith.[89]

More recently, Steven Greer reported that studies by the Law Officers Department and by Boyle, Hadden and Hillyard appeared to confirm the theory that some Loyalists had been perversely acquitted between 1969 and 1973.[90] He went on to say, however, that the Juries (NI) Order 1974, which abolished the property qualification for jury service, had since that time resulted in lists of jurors selected for civil and non-scheduled criminal cases that were randomly selected. This would suggest that such perverse verdicts would be less apt to recur if scheduled offenses were again tried before juries.

Discussing the intimidation of witnesses, Greer reported that one witness in a paramilitary trial had been murdered in 1970, apparently to prevent him from giving evidence and that, between January 1, 1972, and August 31, 1974, 482 witnesses refused to give evidence because of fear.[91] According to Greer, the conventional wisdom was that if witnesses were intimidated, jurors would be intimidated too. As he points out, it is difficult to compel frightened witnesses to testify; but no one has suggested that excusing witnesses from testifying would solve the intimidation problem, since their evidence may be essential. Yet, says Greer, "jury trial was suspended without any comparable evidence of intimidation at all."[92]

The Committee on the Administration of Justice has recently asserted that "insufficient justification for the abolition of jury trial was shown in 1973, and . . . many of the considerations which were relied

---

[89] S. C. Greer and A. White, *Abolishing the Diplock Courts*. London: The Cobden Trust, 1986. Page 78.

[90] Steven C. Greer, *The Diplock Courts*, page 5.

[91] *Ibid.*, page 6.

[92] *Ibid.*

upon can no longer be shown to be relevant."[93] Liberty (The National Council for Civil Liberties) in London concurs: "In fact there was remarkably little evidence to justify either of these worries."[94]

It is not possible to reach a firm conclusion about the basis for the initial decision to introduce Diplock courts without access to government documents that we have not had. Nevertheless, it seems probative that several respected studies have questioned the basis for the decision.

Turning to the present use of Diplock courts, the Helsinki Watch mission in January 1991 found opinion divided as to whether jury trials could safely be resumed.

Brendan Kearney, a lawyer who has practiced for 16 years in London/Derry representing both Loyalists and Republicans charged with acts of terrorism, told us:

> The jury system would be entirely inappropriate at this
> stage because of perverse verdicts. You would get a
> three to one verdict against a Republican in Belfast and
> the opposite here.

Rory McShane, a lawyer practicing in Newry, told the mission that he sees no alternative to the Diplock courts; jury intimidation would occur "without doubt." He reported that juries, largely Protestant, would be intimidated by Protestant paramilitaries from convicting Protestants and would regularly convict Catholics. He believes that the emergency legislation, although he deplores it, is necessary because of the "campaign of terror" that currently afflicts the country.

Sir Oliver Napier, the chairman of the Standing Advisory Commission on Human Rights, told the Helsinki Watch mission that he

---

[93] "A Briefing Paper on the Northern Ireland (Emergency Provisions) Bill," Committee on the Administration of Justice, Belfast, December 1990.

[94] "The Diplock Courts and Restoration of Jury Trial in Northern Ireland," Chapter 2 in draft of a work on Northern Ireland. London: NCCL, December 1990. Page 1.

is not in favor of jury trials involving paramilitary groups; he is afraid that juries will be prejudiced against defendants.

Drew Nelson, an Ulster Unionist Party councillor from South Down, told us there ought not to be juries in terrorist cases because of the danger of perverse verdicts--both in acquittals and in convictions--and the danger of intimidation of witnesses.

On the other hand, Seamus Treacy, a Belfast lawyer, said that he believed there had been no real evidence at the time the Diplock courts were set up that jurors had been intimidated. Treacy stated that it's now possible to avoid a jury composed entirely of Protestants, which was part of the problem in the early 1970's. He supports a move toward more jury trials.

Dr. Joe Hendron, a West Belfast SDLP councillor, said that the SDLP supports a return to jury trials. He believes there was little evidence of perverse verdicts or juror intimidation at the time of the creation of the non-jury system. He said that in sensitive gangster trials in England there has been intensive protection for both jurors and witnesses; he believes the same thing could be done in Northern Ireland.

Helsinki Watch is deeply concerned about the use of Diplock courts. While not recommending their total abolition at this time, Helsinki Watch strongly urges the Northern Ireland authorities to reconsider their use in the light of suggestions that have been made as to how to provide fair trial by jury to defendants and also to protect jurors who hear cases involving paramilitaries. First, juries for scheduled offenses could be democratised, as juries for other offenses were democratised by the Juries (NI) Order 1974. Second, random selection of jurors could be increased. Third, jurors' identities could be concealed. With respect to this recommendation, the following suggestions by Steven Greer should be considered:

> * Jury panels for scheduled offense trials should be drawn from all of Northern Ireland, and such trials, as at present, tried in Belfast;

* A jury panel room should be provided for scheduled offense cases, separated from other members of the public;

* Jurors should be called by number and not by name;

* The jury box, jury panel room and the areas in between should be concealed from the public;

* To protect jurors from a greater risk of being identified because of the length of a large trial, no more than seven defendants should be tried together; and

* Jurors should be screened from the public and the press during trials, visible only to lawyers, defendants and the judge.[95]

---

[95] In "The Diplock Courts and the Restoration of Jury Trial in Northern Ireland," Chapter 2 in draft of a work on Northern Ireland. London: NCCL, December 1990. Pages 6-9.

In *Abolishing the Diplock Courts (supra)*, pages 79 and 80), Greer and White made other suggestions:
* Lawyers for the defense and prosecution should never have access to jury lists;
* Prospective jurors need not know until they arrive at the courthouse whether they have been called for a scheduled or a non-scheduled case;
* As far as possible, one Loyalist and one Republican trial should be carried on simultaneously, to further confuse anyone who wished to interfere with a juror;
* Jury foremen should not be required to disclose whether a verdict was unanimous or by a majority;
* A mini-bus should be made available to take jurors from the court to the center of Belfast and deposit them at different stops each day, the stops to be chosen by the driver;
* Court administrators should "look favorably" on applications to be excused from jury duty from people living in sections of Northern Ireland where paramilitaries exercise a good deal of influence;
* Jurors who have served in a scheduled offense trial should be excused from further jury duty.

Helsinki Watch recommends a gradual resumption of jury trials for a reduced list of scheduled offenses in Northern Ireland. Non-jury trials should be used only in cases in which there appears to be a significant risk of jury intimidation and perverse verdicts; the burden should be on the government to demonstrate that such a risk exists. All other cases should be heard by juries. As a step toward reducing the number of cases tried in Diplock courts, Helsinki Watch recommends that the scheduling-out process should be reversed. That is, the Attorney General should, instead of "scheduling out" inappropriate cases, be required to "schedule in" cases in which political violence played a part. If a defendant objects to the government's certification, a hearing should be required in which the government would bear the burden of demonstrating that the case involved terrorism and that jury intimidation would be likely. A jury trial would be held unless specific evidence indicated the need for a trial before a judge alone. If intimidation occurred during a trial, the case would then be heard by a judge without a jury. Finally, the defendant should have the right to waive a jury trial.

The view that the number of non-jury trials should be reduced is consistent with the judgment of many commentators. For example, Sir Oliver Napier, chairman of the Standing Advisory Commission on Human Rights, told the Helsinki Watch mission that the SACHR believes that the number of scheduled offenses is "unrealistically large." The SACHR has recommended a "scheduling in" approach and further suggests that the Attorney General schedule in only cases in which he believes there is a risk of intimidation of witnesses or jurors or that the interests of justice require such a step.

Helsinki Watch believes that reducing the number of scheduled offenses and requiring the Attorney General to schedule in cases involving political violence rather than to schedule out cases that do not, would be positive steps toward restoring trial by jury in Northern Ireland until such time as jury trials are resumed for all defendants, consistent with long tradition in the United Kingdom.[96]

---

[96] Another troublesome issue in Diplock courts is the admissibility of confessions. Confessions are admitted into evidence more easily in non-jury trials in Diplock courts than they are in courts in which juries hear cases. For a full discussion of the standards used for the admissibility of confessions, see the

Cases Alleging Miscarriage of Justice

Since 1989, verdicts in three cases involving terrorist bombings have been overturned in Great Britain. In all three cases, defendants from Northern Ireland were convicted by juries of offenses committed in Great Britain; the convictions were found "unsafe" because of the behavior of police officers and questions concerning forensic evidence used in the trials. All three cases have received a great deal of publicity, and have raised serious questions about the criminal justice system in Britain.

In the first, the Higher Appellate Court in October 1989 overturned the convictions of "The Guildford Four," who had been convicted of a terrorist bombing and given life sentences in 1975. In the "Maguire Seven," a related case, the Home Secretary ruled in June 1990 that the convictions could not stand; an independent inquiry had raised doubts about the forensic evidence used in the case. The seven defendants had already completed their sentences.

In the most recent case, the "Birmingham Six," six men were exonerated on March 14, 1991, after serving 16 years in prison for a deadly terrorist bombing in Birmingham. The prosecutors had conceded that much of the evidence against the men had been fabricated by police and forensic experts. In the uproar surrounding the men's exoneration, then-Home Secretary Kenneth Baker announced the formation of a royal commission that will undertake a sweeping two-year review of the criminal justice system in Great Britain.

Questions have been raised as to whether such miscarriages of justice have taken place in the Diplock courts in Northern Ireland. In its 1987 report, *Criminal Justice and Human Rights in Northern Ireland,* the Committee on International Human Rights of the Association of the Bar of the City of New York concluded that the use of non-jury trials in Diplock courts had not resulted in wrongful convictions. The report stated:

---

material on interrogation in Chapter II above.

95

One baseline measure of the fairness of a judicial system (but not necessarily the only one) is whether it produces wrongful convictions--convictions of innocent persons or convictions of ostensibly guilty persons but not based on the evidence in a given case. Consequently, in every interview which we conducted we sought that information. Not one person to whom we spoke, however, directed our attention to a single case in which there existed a belief that a factually erroneous conviction had occurred. Certainly, the absence of such a claim by even the severest critics of a court system helps to reduce the degree of disquiet that one might have about the administration of justice in a state of emergency.[97]

The Bar Association's statement was referred to by several people in Northern Ireland, including Lord Chief Justice Brian Hutton, as evidence that the Diplock court system is fair to defendants.

Some defense lawyers with whom we spoke in Northern Ireland did not share this view. A lawyer who has practiced for 16 years in London/Derry, for example, and who has represented both Republicans and Loyalists, told us that he believed that some people were wrongly convicted; he estimated that about one conviction in one hundred was of an innocent person. An Ulster Unionist Party representative told us that he believed that "a certain number of innocent people have been convicted under the present system." An SDLP councillor in Belfast told us that he believed there had been many perverse judgments in the 1970's, but that he believed that most, but not all, convictions now are "safe."

One of the two best-known cases at present in Northern Ireland in which a miscarriage of justice has been alleged is the case of the UDR Four. In November 1983, a young Armagh man, Adrian Carroll, was

---

[97] Hellerstein, McKay and Schlam, *Criminal Justice and Human Rights in Northern Ireland, supra*, page 56.

shot and killed in an alley in Armagh. Carroll's family were known to be Republicans; his murder was claimed by the Protestant Action Force. Six members of an Ulster Defense Regiment (UDR) patrol were subsequently charged with Carroll's death on the basis of confessions which they later claimed were obtained by police brutality and trickery. Four were found guilty and given life sentences; their conviction was upheld on appeal in November 1987.

All four, Winston Allen, Noel Bell, Jim Hagan and Neil Latimer, have steadily denied their guilt. Questions have been raised about the way their confessions were obtained, about the reliability of a witness against them, and about other evidence. In January 1991, a committee formed to fight for their release prepared an extensive dossier arguing the men's innocence. This information was turned over to Secretary of State Peter Brooke with a request that he evaluate whether there are grounds to refer the case to the Appeal Court so that it, in turn, could consider whether a re-trial should be ordered.

Margaret and Norman Bell, the parents of Noel Bell, one of the four UDR men, told the Helsinki Watch mission that Noel was picked up by police at 4:00 a.m. on a Friday, and signed a confession early on Sunday morning. Noel was interrogated for many hours, including during the hours between 10:00 p.m. and 2:00 a.m., although police rules forbid interrogations after midnight. Noel told his parents, and the court, that he had been punched in the chest and testicles and had fallen to the ground. His lawyer produced medical evidence in court showing bruises on his body. Noel told the court that he had had such a rough time at the hands of the police that he would have signed anything.

The second case to receive considerable attention as a possible miscarriage of justice case is actually a series of cases stemming from the killing of two British Army corporals on Andersonstown Road near Casement Park in Belfast on March 12, 1988. Earlier, on March 6, 1988, members of the British Army Special Air Services (SAS) had shot and killed three unarmed members of the IRA in Gibraltar. Amnesty International and others called for a full inquiry into the killings.

As the three victims of the Gibraltar shootings were being buried in Belfast, a Loyalist gunman, Michael Stone, launched a gun and grenade attack on the mourners. Three men were shot dead, and more than thirty people injured. One of the dead mourners was Caoimhin MacBradaigh.

During Caoimhin MacBradaigh's funeral on March 12, 1988, two British corporals in plain clothes drove into the funeral cortege. Their car was surrounded by mourners and the soldiers left their car; one fired a gun into the air. The two soldiers were overpowered by the crowd, taken away from the cortege and shot and killed.

Forty people have been charged with offenses arising from the incident. The offenses and the numbers charged are:

* murder (8)
* grievous bodily harm (20)
* false imprisonment (16)
* causing an affray (8)
* conspiracy to pervert the course of justice (2)

A Casement Accused Relatives Committee with whom Helsinki Watch met in Belfast was formed to bring attention to what relatives consider a miscarriage of justice; they allege that all 40 are innocent of murder. None of the 40 has been charged with membership in the IRA. According to the committee, the defendants were acting in self-defense, as they were terrified that the soldiers were about to repeat the attack by Michael Stone. So far, five of the 40 have been sentenced to life imprisonment for murder, although the prosecution acknowledged that none possessed firearms or fired the fatal shots. One defendant was given a 15-year sentence for false imprisonment; the prosecution acknowledged that his involvement was limited to events that took place at the soldiers' car. His sentence was quashed on November 16, 1990; the Lord Chief Justice ruled that the conviction was unsafe and unsatisfactory. Ten men are awaiting trial.

The Committee on the Administration of Justice (CAJ) has compiled a list of six other cases in which wrongful convictions have been alleged and campaigns have been set up to work for re-trial or release. These are the cases of:

* Thomas Green, convicted of murder in 1986 and sentenced to life. The conviction was based solely on

Green's confession, which he claims he gave because of ill-treatment by police during interrogation at the Castlereagh Police Station.

* Peter McClay, convicted of murder in 1987 and given a life sentence. He alleges that police ill-treatment made him sign a confession. He was not able to prove ill-treatment in court, but a co-defendant was successful in doing so and the charges against him were dropped.

* William Bell, sentenced to life for murder in March 1989. Bell alleges that police mistreatment of his sister in Gough Barracks (she was being questioned about the same offense as Bell) caused her to break down completely. He alleges that he confessed in order to make police leave his sister alone. He claims to have alibi witnesses who were not called at his trial.

* Walter McAllister, who claims he signed a confession under duress in Castlereagh in April 1989. When the case came to trial a plea bargain resulted, and McAllister agreed to plead guilty to lesser charges of conspiracy and being an accessory to murder. He received a six year sentence, and should be released in a year or so.

* Brian McLernon, convicted of possession of weapons in December 1990. Alleging innocence, McLernon exercised his right to remain silent. His co-defendants, who made statements, received 9 year sentences; McLernon received 18 years.

* Barry Murray, convicted in 1990 and sentenced to 18 years on the basis of an uncorroborated verbal admission. He alleges that police notes of his interrogation were altered to make it appear that he had made a confession. He denies doing so, and maintains his innocence. His case is on appeal.

Helsinki Watch has no way of knowing whether any of these men have been wrongfully convicted. Their cases, and the cases of the UDR

Four and the Casement Accused, are reported only to show that questions have been raised about the fairness of the Diplock courts in Northern Ireland and, particularly, whether miscarriages of justice exist that are similar to the three cases in Great Britain in which longstanding verdicts have been overturned.

Threats Against Lawyers

The Helsinki Watch mission was told of a disturbing rise in the number of threats made against lawyers who represent defendants in political violence cases. These threats have increased since the 1989 murder of Patrick Finucane, a leading human rights lawyer. Lawyers, both Protestant and Catholic, are threatened by anonymous telephone calls and unsigned letters, as well as threats made by police to lawyers' clients during interrogation.[98]

Patrick Finucane was killed in his home in front of his wife and children on February 12, 1989. He was shot twice through a glass door and twelve more times as he lay on the floor. A Loyalist group, the Ulster Freedom Fighters, claimed credit for his murder; no one has been charged with the act. He was the first solicitor killed in Northern Ireland since 1969. The president of the Law Society of Northern Ireland called the murder "a shocking attack on the whole system of justice."

Pat Finucane, who was 39 when he was killed, represented both Republicans and Loyalists accused of terrorist actions. He also represented families of victims of plastic bullets and people unlawfully arrested by the British Army or the RUC; he defended free speech and association and took cases to the House of Lords and to the European Court of Human Rights. He was involved in the inquests into some of the 1982 deaths which were later investigated by John Stalker (see Chapter IV).

In 1988, Pat Finucane won the release of a client, Brian Gillen, from Castlereagh Holding Centre by presenting medical evidence that showed mistreatment in detention. Brian Gillen reported to Amnesty

---

[98] *In Defense of Rights: Attacks on Lawyers and Judges in 1990.* Lawyers Committee for Human Rights, New York, 1991, p. 155.

International on his release that during his interrogation threats were made by the RUC that the solicitor who represented him would be shot by Loyalist paramilitaries. This was just over a year before Pat Finucane's death.

Shortly before his death, Mr. Finucane successfully defended a client charged with the murder of a British soldier on Andersonstown Road in Belfast in 1988 (one of the Casement Accused; see section above, "Cases Alleging Miscarriage of Justice"). The case received wide publicity.

Three weeks before Mr. Finucane was shot, on January 17, 1989, Douglas Hogg, a lawyer and Home Office Minister, said in Parliament: "There are in Northern Ireland a number of solicitors who are unduly sympathetic to the cause of the IRA . . . I state it on the basis of advice that I have received, guidance that I have been given by people who are dealing in these matters." Hogg was sharply criticized by many who felt that his words could stimulate violence against lawyers who were fulfilling their responsibilities in representing accused persons in the courts--the phenomenon of identifying the lawyer with the cause of the clients he represents. An International Delegation of Lawyers asserted that his words may have "played a part in creating a climate in which the likelihood of the murder of Pat Finucane or another lawyer was increased."[99]

Peter Madden, who was Pat Finucane's partner for the ten years before his murder, told the Helsinki Watch mission that the campaign against solicitors has increased since the Brian Gillen case. Mr. Madden and his law partner, Kevin Winters, said that of 65 cases during 1990, two clients had received blatant death threats against Madden and/or Winters, and in 38 other cases police had verbally abused the solicitors. Verbal abuse included referring to one of the lawyers as "stupid," disparaging the solicitor, sometimes on a sectarian basis, telling the client the lawyer was in it only for the money and didn't care what happened to the client, and

---

[99] *Legal Defense in Northern Ireland, Report of an International Delegation of Lawyers.* Summer, 1989. Page 20.

saying "I bet Madden is shitting himself over what happened to Pat Finucane; he thinks it will happen to him."[100]

Asked about the effect that death threats have had on him, Mr. Madden said that he tries not to think about them. Mr. Winters said, "You try to get the job done. You can't let it get to you--you could get paranoid, and that would ruin the effectiveness of your work." Both have taken security precautions at their homes and in the office.

Mr. Madden told us that "with Pat, we didn't treat the death threats as seriously as we should have --it just hadn't happened before." Mr. Madden believes that some of the threats and abuse occur because some police see lawyers as a threat--"an extension of the IRA-- not just lawyers doing the job we're trained to do."

Madden and Winters have notified the Law Society, which is the governing body for solicitors, of death threats. "The Law Society told us that it is a political matter, to be taken up with 'your political party.'"

Alex Attwood, an attorney and an SDLP councillor in Belfast, told us that the legal profession in general has "opted out of civil rights in Northern Ireland. It took the Law Society twenty years of civil rights abuses to form a Human Rights Committee, and that was only after Pat Finucane's killing. Most barristers take no stand on human rights."

Brendan Kearney, a lawyer who practices in London/Derry, told the Helsinki Watch mission that police often tell his clients that he is "an IRA solicitor, and that solicitors are seen as worse than terrorists, because they are abetting terrorists and also making money out of it. Defense lawyers are definitely under pressure; we're on the firing line. Police regard us as security risks. One of my clients told me that he was told by a police officer that I am an intelligence officer for the IRA. It's the old problem of identifying the lawyer with the client." He, too, has taken security precautions.

---

[100] See Appendix I for a series of statements given to Madden and Winters that included threats against, or disparaging remarks about the lawyers by police during interrogation of clients. Peter Madden told the Helsinki Watch mission that this is only a partial list of such statements.

Andrew Puddephat, the director of Liberty in London, told us that he believes that threats to solicitors are a "threat to the heart of the criminal justice system."

* * *

International agreements provide standards for the treatment of lawyers. The UN Draft Principles on the Role of Lawyers approved by the Eighth UN Congress on the Prevention of Crime and the Treatment of Offenders (August 1990) provides guarantees for the functioning of lawyers:

> 16. Governments shall ensure that lawyers (a) are able to perform all of their professional functions without intimidation, hindrance, harassment or improper interference . . .
>
> 17. Where the security of lawyers is threatened as a result of discharging their functions, they shall be adequately safeguarded by the authorities.
>
> 18. Lawyers shall not be identified with their clients or their clients' causes as a result of discharging their functions.

The Concluding Document of the Copenhagen Meeting of the Conference on the Human Dimension of the CSCE (June 1990) states in paragraph 5.13:

> The independence of legal practitioners will be recognized and protected, in particular as regards conditions for recruitment and practice.

There is substantial credible evidence that members of the legal profession in Northern Ireland who represent defendants in political violence cases are subjected to threats and harassment. The murder of Patrick Finucane indicates that such threats cannot be taken lightly. The rule of law requires that people accused of criminal acts receive skilled and independent legal representation. Helsinki Watch believes that in the volatile situation that exists in Northern Ireland today lawyers carrying out their responsibilities to defend clients accused of terrorist acts are in a dangerous position.

Helsinki Watch urges lawyers to report threats to the authorities and urges bar associations to take such threats seriously and to provide support for lawyers whose personal safety has been threatened. Helsinki Watch also recommends that special efforts be made to protect lawyers and to guarantee that they can represent clients without interference, harassment or intimidation. Slurs and threats against lawyers should be thoroughly investigated; if police are found to have engaged in such threats, appropriate disciplinary action should be taken.

VI. THE USE OF FORCE BY PARAMILITARY GROUPS

As previously noted, almost 2,900 people have been killed since 1969 in connection with political violence in Northern Ireland. More than three quarters of these have been killed by paramilitary groups. This appalling loss of life is a major human rights problem in Northern Ireland.

The Helsinki Watch mission examined the question of the use of force by paramilitary groups in Northern Ireland and concluded that the use of such force is in violation of customary international humanitarian law.

The Irish Republican Army (IRA)

The IRA is an illegal Republican paramilitary group;[101] it was outlawed by the Northern Ireland (Emergency Provisions) Act of 1973 (EPA), along with six other organizations.[102]   The Irish National Liberation Army (INLA), another Republican paramilitary group, was added to the list of proscribed organizations in 1978.

The membership of the IRA is thought to be in the hundreds, but the exact number is unknown. The IRA's aims are the withdrawal of the British and the re-unification of Ireland. The IRA targets individuals such as police, soldiers, prison officials, judges, business leaders, and people thought to be collaborators with or informers for the security forces or for Loyalist paramilitaries. The IRA has also firebombed or otherwise attacked institutions and business premises, such as shopping malls, and has killed or wounded civilians who are not associated with paramilitaries.

---

[101] The group now known as the IRA is actually the "Provisional IRA", or "Provos," which broke away from the "Official IRA" in 1970.

[102] The other proscribed organizations were Cumann na mBan, Fianna na hEireann, The Red Hand Commando, Saor Eire, The Ulster Freedom Fighters and the Ulster Volunteer Force. EPA, Schedule 2.

Because the IRA believes that it is fighting a war against an illegal occupation,[103] it claims credit for its acts of violence. According to the Irish Information Partnership, Republican paramilitaries (the IRA and the INLA) were responsible for 1608 -- or 57.7 percent -- of the 2,786 deaths related to the "war" that occurred in Northern Ireland between 1969 and 1989. Of these killings, 847 (52.7 percent) were of security force members and 574 (35.7 percent) were of civilians. Of the civilian casualties, 173 (10.8 percent) were Catholic, 379 (23.6 percent) Protestant, and 22 (1.4 percent) other.

During the same time period, Republican paramilitaries also killed 18 Loyalist paramilitaries (1.1 percent of the total number of people they killed), 146 of their own members (9.1 percent) and 23 prison officers.

In 1990, the IRA was responsible for 44 of the total of 76 people killed; 12 were RUC members, eight UDR, and seven were soldiers in the regular army. Five men were killed because they allegedly worked for or provided supplies for the authorities; two were killed as informers. The IRA killed eight civilians as well. Another Republican paramilitary group, the Irish People's Liberation Organization (IPLO), which was banned during the year, killed two Protestants whom they described as Loyalist extremists.

In particularly gruesome attacks on October 24, 1990, the IRA killed seven people--six soldiers and one civilian--by using as "human bombs" three Catholic civilians, described as "collaborators" with the security forces. Fourteen soldiers, two policemen and at least 21 civilians were wounded in the attacks. In each attack, IRA members took over a house, held the family hostage, and forced a male member of the family to drive a vehicle loaded with explosives to targets in London/Derry, Newry, and Omagh. The drivers were strapped into the vehicles and timers were set to detonate the bombs; two of the drivers escaped, but

---

[103] The Green Book, the IRA's training manual and rule book, states the movement's aims: " ... the Irish Republican Army, its leadership, is the lawful government of the Irish Republic; all other parliaments or assemblies claiming the right to speak for and to pass laws on behalf of the Irish people are illegal assemblies, puppet governments of an occupying force."

one, Patsy Gillespie, a married man with three children who worked as a kitchen assistant for the Ministry of Defense, was killed. The second man worked at an Army base in Omagh; the third was a 65-year-old garage owner who was said to have sold goods to police officers.[104]

In some of the other violent incidents that took place during 1990, the IRA killed four soldiers in a bomb attack on a two-vehicle British Army patrol about 30 miles south of Belfast on April 9. On July 24, the IRA killed a Roman Catholic nun and three police officers; the RUC car ran over and detonated an explosive device near Armagh--the nun and another woman were driving in a car going in the opposite direction.

The IRA has killed and wounded people outside of Northern Ireland. In 1983, a car bomb outside of Harrod's killed five people and wounded 91. Eleven others were killed in London between 1979 and 1988. During that period, Member of Parliament Airey Neave was killed by the INLA. In 1984, the IRA tried to kill Prime Minister Margaret Thatcher and other members of her Cabinet by bombing the Grand Hotel in Brighton; five people were killed and 30 injured.

In 1990, five bombings took place in London; two soldiers were killed and 15 other people were wounded. On July 30, 1990, the IRA killed Conservative Member of Parliament Ian Gow by planting a bomb in his car outside his home, 40 miles southeast of London. On February 7, 1991, the IRA lobbed mortars at 10 Downing Street while a Cabinet meeting was in session, presided over by Prime Minister John Major; there were no casualties. Eleven days later, the IRA claimed responsibility for killing one person and wounding 40 in bombing attacks on Victoria and Paddington Stations during the early morning.[105]

A total of 296 members of the IRA or the INLA were killed between 1969 and 1989. One hundred twenty-three (41.6 percent) were

---

[104] *The Independent* and *The New York Times*, October 24 and 26, 1990.

[105] *The New York Times*, February 8, 19 and 20, 1991; *The Independent*, January 2, 1991.

killed by security forces, 21 (7.1 percent) by Loyalist paramilitaries, 4 by others, and 146 (49.3 percent) by their own members or by themselves, frequently in bombings that went wrong.

The IRA has also carried out frequent knee-cappings, or "punishment shootings" against civilians. In some parts of Northern Ireland, the Helsinki Watch mission was told, normal policing has broken down, partly because local people have lost confidence in the police and do not want to report crimes, and partly because some areas are felt to be too dangerous for police to enter without army guards. In these areas, paramilitary groups have taken on a quasi-police role. According to the Northern Ireland Office, between 1973 and December 1990, 1021 people were wounded, many severely, by such punishment shootings. In these shootings, there is no formal trial and no judicial review or appeal.

Loyalist Paramilitary Groups

Loyalist paramilitary groups, including the Ulster Volunteer Force (UVF) and the Ulster Freedom Fighters (UFF) (both banned by the EPA since 1973) as well as the Ulster Defense Association (UDA), also engage in and claim credit for violent acts. According to the Irish Information Partnership, "Loyalist paramilitaries," Unionists who support the use of violence to maintain union with the UK, killed 705 people between 1969 and 1989. (See Table III in Chapter III.) That represents 25.3 percent of the total number of people killed during that time. The vast majority of these killings, 632, or 89.6 percent, were civilians, of whom 506 were Catholic, 114 Protestant, and 12 other.

Loyalist groups also killed 10 members of security forces, 21 members of the IRA or the INLA, 40 of their own members and two prison officers.

Loyalists frequently target suspected members of the IRA. They also engage in sectarian, or "tit-for-tat" killings: typically, if a Protestant is killed, Loyalists go to a Catholic neighborhood and kill a Catholic at random, for revenge. Loyalist paramilitaries killed 19 people in 1990, many in retaliation for IRA killings. Four of the deaths were of Protestants, two of whom were said to be informers; two were killed accidentally. The fifteen other victims were Catholics who the Loyalists claim had IRA connections, but only two have been acknowledged as IRA members.[106]

Loyalist killings have continued this year. On March 4, 1991, the Ulster Volunteer Force took reponsibility for shooting and killing four Catholic men and wounding a fifth at a village pub in Cappagh, 50 miles west of Belfast. The UVF said: "This was not a sectarian attack on the Catholic community, but was an operation directed at the very roots of the Provisional IRA command structure in the Armagh-Tyrone area."[107]

On March 29, 1991, a group called the Protestant Action Force claimed responsibility for shooting and killing two Catholic teenagers, Eileen Duffy, 19, and Katrina Rennie, 16, and a 29-year-old man, Brian Frizell, in a candy van on March 28th. The group asserted that Ms. Duffy and the owner of the candy van supported Republicanism, and said that the attack was in revenge for the wounding on March 21 of Margaret Cooke, who works for the RUC in London/Derry. "We warn the public to stay away from all businesses owned and staffed by known Republicans," the group said.[108]

According to the Irish Information Partnership, a total of 73 Loyalist paramilitaries were killed between 1969 and 1989; 13 by security forces, 18 by Nationalist paramilitaries, two by unknown assailants, and, as stated above, 40 by their own members. The total of 73 killed is 2.6 percent of the total killings that took place during the 21-year period. Although only 73 Loyalists were killed, Loyalists themselves killed 705 people during that time.

Loyalists, too, use punishment shootings. According to the Northern Ireland Office, Loyalists carried out 553 (35 percent) of the 1574 punishment shootings that took place between 1973 and December 31, 1990.

---

[106] *The Independent*, January 2, 1991.

[107] *The New York Times*, March 5, 1991.

[108] *The New York Times*, March 30, 1991.

International Humanitarian Law Standards

International humanitarian law--the laws of war--have as a central concern the victims of armed conflicts. The four Geneva Conventions of 1949 cover not only international armed conflicts, but also, in Article 3, common to all four conventions, internal armed conflicts.

Common Article 3 requires that civilians be treated humanely, without regard to religion or other criteria.[109] It specifically prohibits

---

[109] Common Article 3 states:

In the case of armed conflict not of an international character occurring in the territory of one of the High Contracting Parties, each Party to the conflict shall be bound to apply, as a minimum, the following provisions:

(1) Persons taking no active part in the hostilities, including members of armed forces who have laid down their arms and those placed *hors de combat* by sickness, wounds, detention, or any other cause, shall in all circumstances be treated humanely, without any adverse distinction founded on race, colour, religion or faith, sex, birth or wealth, or any other similar criteria.

To this end, the following acts are and shall remain prohibited at any time and in any place whatsoever with respect to the above-mentioned persons:

(a) violence to life and person, in particular murder of all kinds, mutilation, cruel treatment and torture;
(b) taking of hostages;
(c) outrages upon personal dignity, in particular humiliating and degrading treatment;
(d) the passing of sentences and the carrying out of executions without previous judgement pronounced by a regularly constituted court, affording all the judicial guarantees which are recognized as indispensable by civilized peoples.

(2) The wounded and sick shall be collected and cared for.

An impartial humanitarian body, such as the International Committee of the Red Cross, may offer its services to the Parties to the conflict.

The Parties to the conflict should further endeavour to bring into force, by means of special agreements, all or part of the other provisions of the present Convention.

The application of the preceding provisions shall not affect the legal

110

murder, cruel treatment, torture, and humiliating or degrading treatment. It also forbids the passing of sentences and carrying out of executions without a previous judgment by a recognized court and without due process of law. Common Article 3 is binding on all parties to the conflict, government and opposition forces.

The application of Common Article 3 to the conflict in Northern Ireland is debatable. Common Article 3 does not define internal armed conflict. Nor does it define the level of violence required to invoke the protection of the Article. Commentary on the Article suggests that organized armed groups in control of substantial territory would be covered:

> The conflicts referred to in Article 3 are armed conflicts, with armed forces on either side engaged in hostilities-- conflicts, in short, which are in many respects similar to an international war, but take place within the confines of a single country. In many cases, each of the Parties is in possession of a portion of the national territory and there is often some sort of front.[110]

There is no "front" in the Northern Ireland conflict. Neither the IRA nor the Loyalist paramilitaries appear to be "in possession of a portion of national territory," although it has been argued that the IRA controls some border areas, especially South Armagh.[111]

---

status of the Parties to the conflict.

[110] "Commentary to the Geneva Conventions of 12 August 1949, Geneva Convention Relative to the Protection of Civilian Persons in Time of War," Geneva, International Committee of the Red Cross, J. Pictet, ed., 1958, p. 36.

[111] Protocol II to the 1949 Geneva Conventions, which supplements Common Article 3, applies only to armed conflicts "which take place in the territory of a High Contracting Party between its armed forces and dissident armed forces or other organized armed groups which, under responsible command, exercise such control over a part of its territory as to enable them to carry out sustained and concerted military operations and to implement this Protocol." The Protocol does not apply to "situations of internal disturbances and tensions, such as riots, isolated and sporadic acts of violence and other acts of a

In 1986 the International Court of Justice stated in a judgment on a case concerning military and paramilitary activities in and against Nicaragua that the rules defined in Common Article 3

> also constitute a minimum yardstick, in addition to the more elaborate rules which are also to apply to international conflicts; and that they are rules which . . . reflect what the Court in 1949 called "elementary considerations of humanity." [112]

The International Committee of the Red Cross (ICRC), citing this decision, stated that "the general rule of international humanitarian law is therefore seen as a standard of behaviour expressing a general, basic principle of conduct which underlies all international humanitarian law."[113] Moreover, as a leading scholar of humanitarian law has pointed out, "the norms stated in Article 3(1)(a)-(c) are of such an elementary, ethical character, and echo so many provisions in other humanitarian and human rights treaties, that they must be regarded as embodying minimum standards of customary law."[114] According to

---

similar nature, as not being armed conflicts."

[112] International Court of Justice, *Reports of Judgments, Advisory Opinions and Orders.* Nicaragua v. United States of America. Merits, Judgment of 27 June 1986, p. 114, para. 218. Cited in *International Review of the Red Cross*, International Committee of the Red Cross, September-October 1990, page 386.

[113] *International Review of the Red Cross, op.cit.*, page 386.

[114] Theodor Meron, *Human Rights and Humanitarian Norms as Customary Law*, Clarendon Press, Oxford, 1989, p. 34. These provisions prohibit murder, mutilation, cruel treatment and torture of non-combatants or those who are *hors de combat*; taking of hostages; and outrages upon personal dignity. Professor Meron writes that "I consider at least the core due process principle in Article 3(1)(d) . . . to embody customary law." *Ibid.*, pp. 34-35. This provision prohibits "the passing of sentences and the carrying out of executions without previous judgment pronounced by a regularly constituted court, affording all the judicial guarantees which are recognized as indispensable by civilized peoples."

these standards, the conflict in Northern Ireland is covered by the principles set forth in Common Article 3 whether or not encompassed by its literal terms.

In another effort to apply humanitarian law principles to internal conflicts that are not covered by Common Article 3, the International Committee of the Red Cross in 1990 issued "Rules of International Humanitarian Law Governing the Conduct of Hostilities in Non-International Armed Conflicts."[115]   Rule 1 distinguishes between combatants and civilians, and states: "The obligation to distinguish between combatants and civilians is a general rule applicable in non-international armed conflicts. It prohibits indiscriminate attacks."

Rule 2 prohibits attacks against civilians individually or collectively in internal armed conflicts, and forbids "acts of violence intended primarily to spread terror among the civilian population."

Rule 6 prohibits attacks on dwellings and other installations used only by the civilian population. The commentary states that such attacks violate the general principle that "the sole purpose of military operations should be to weaken the enemy's military strength."

In Rule 8, on precautionary measures in attacks, the ICRC states: "The general rule to distinguish between combatants and civilians and the prohibition of attacks against the civilian population as such or against individual civilians implies, in order to be effective, that all feasible precautions have to be taken to avoid injury, loss or damage to the civilian population."

Thus, the central concern of agreements and principles concerning internal armed conflicts is the protection of civilians. Yet paramilitary groups on both sides of the Northern Ireland conflict have inflicted hundreds of casualties and deaths on civilians. Republican paramilitaries killed 574 civilians between 1969 and 1989; Loyalist paramilitaries killed 632. In the case of the Loyalists, an overwhelming number of killings, 89.6 percent, were of civilians. For the Republicans, civilians represented 35.7 percent of their total killings. Loyalists, in "tit-

---

[115] *International Review of the Red Cross, op.cit.* Pages 383-408.

for-tat" killings, specifically target civilians. The IRA detonates explosives either in a direct attempt to kill civilians or with utter disregard for human life--for example, in the bomb that killed five people outside of Harrod's in 1983 and wounded 91, and in the bombing attacks on Paddington and Victoria Stations in February 1991 that killed one person and wounded 40.

Helsinki Watch strongly condemns the use of violence by paramilitary groups against civilians in the conflict in Northern Ireland.

The IRA has also taken hostages, an act that is forbidden by Common Article 3 and, in its prohibition against cruel, inhuman or degrading treatment, by the 1990 Declaration of Minimum Humanitarian Standards in internal armed conflicts. In the case of the "human bomb" incidents of October 1990, described earlier, the IRA took three "collaborators" hostage, strapping them into vans loaded with explosives. The group also held hostage the drivers' families. These acts also constitute cruel treatment and torture.

The "punishment shootings" also constitute cruel treatment and torture of civilians in violation of Common Article 3, the Declaration of Minimum Standards, and the ICRC's "Rules of International Humanitarian Law Governing the Conduct of Hostilities in Non-International Armed Conflicts."

Helsinki Watch strongly condemns the taking of hostages and the "punishment shootings" meted out by paramilitary groups in Northern Ireland.

The conflict in Northern Ireland may be described as one of "internal strife," rather than "internal armed conflict." The term "internal strife" is used to describe conflict situations that are below the level of violence required for the applicability of Common Article 3.[116] It is generally used for situations that are not as intense as civil wars or as

---

[116] See Theodor Meron, *Human Rights in Internal Strife, Their International Protection*, Grotius, 1987, pages 71-104, for a discussion of the difficulties in defining "internal strife."

well-organized as armed insurrections, and for situations involving sporadic actions, rather than sustained conflict.

There are as yet no international agreements regarding internal strife. In December 1990, however, the Institute for Human Rights adopted a Declaration of Minimum Humanitarian Standards, drafted by a panel of experts in Humanitarian Law, to be used in such situations.[117] The declaration sets minimum standards applicable in "internal violence, disturbances, tensions, and public emergencies, and which cannot be derogated from under any circumstances . . . whether or not a state of emergency has been proclaimed."

The declaration applies to all parties to a conflict, non-government as well as government forces, and would therefore apply to both Republican and Loyalist paramilitary groups, as well as to security forces in Northern Ireland. Article 3 of the Declaration requires that all persons be treated humanely, and prohibits "murder, torture, mutilation, rape, as well as cruel, inhuman or degrading treatment or punishment and other outrages upon personal dignity." It also forbids collective punishments and the taking of hostages. Article 6 prohibits "Acts or threats of violence the primary purpose or foreseeable effect of which is to spread terror among the population."

*　*　*

Since 1969, paramilitary groups in Northern Ireland have killed members of security forces and members of opposing paramilitary groups as well as civilians. These killings may of course be prosecuted in accordance with the criminal laws in effect in Northern Ireland.

As to the applicability of international humanitarian law to such killings, Protocol I of the Geneva Conventions, which applies to international armed conflicts including "armed conflicts in which peoples

---

[117] *Declaration of Minimum Humanitarian Standards*, adopted by a meeting of experts convened by the Institute for Human Rights, Abo Akademi University, in Turku/Abo, Finland, 30 November-2 December 1990.

are fighting against colonial domination and alien occupation," states in Article 37 that:

It is prohibited to kill, injure or capture an adversary by resort to perfidy.

Article 37 goes on to provide examples of perfidy, including:

(c) the feigning of civilian, non-combatant status.

In the political violence in Northern Ireland, members of paramilitary groups do not wear uniforms, do not bear arms openly, and frequently kill by assassination. Such killings may be properly characterized as being carried out "by resort to perfidy."

Protocol I may not be strictly applicable to the conflict in Northern Ireland: Britain has not ratified Protocol I, and it is beyond the mandate of Helsinki Watch to judge whether this conflict involves a fight against colonial domination. Nevertheless, Protocol I embodies a principle of customary international law of general application. Helsinki Watch calls attention to the fact that many of the killings of members of the security forces and members of opposing paramilitary groups in Northern Ireland take place in disregard of this principle.

Helsinki Watch condemns the use of violence by paramilitary groups against security forces and opposing paramilitary groups in violation of the principles underlying customary international humanitarian law.

VII. FREEDOM OF MOVEMENT

Exclusion Orders

The Prevention of Terrorism Act gives the Secretary of State the authority to issue orders excluding from Northern Ireland, from Great Britain, or from all of the United Kingdom, people suspected of involvement in terrorism.[118]   Terrorism is defined as "the use of violence for political ends, and includes any use of violence for the purpose of putting the public or any section of the public in fear" (Section 20(1)).

Specifically, Section 5 of the PTA, which deals with excluding people from Great Britain, provides that

(1) If the Secretary of State is satisfied that any person--

(a) is or has been concerned in the commission, preparation or instigation of acts of terrorism to which this Part of the Act applies; or

(b) is attempting or may attempt to enter Great Britain with a view to being concerned in the commission, preparation or instigation of such acts of terrorism, the Secretary of State must make an exclusion order against him.

An exclusion order under this section prohibits a person from being in, or entering, Great Britain. An order cannot be issued against someone who is a British citizen and "is at the time ordinarily resident in Great Britain and has [been so] . . . throughout the last three years"; or who has been ordered excluded from Northern Ireland.

---

[118]   The Secretary of State for Northern Ireland exercises this power in relation to people in, or seeking to enter, Northern Ireland. The UK Home Secretary exercises the power in relation to those within or seeking entrance to Great Britain or other parts of the UK.

Section 6, which deals with excluding people from Northern Ireland, sets forth the same criteria. It also states that British citizens cannot be excluded if they ordinarily live in Northern Ireland and have done so for the past three years, or if they have been excluded from Great Britain under Section 5.

Section 7 of the Act gives the Secretary of State the power to exclude from all of the United Kingdom anyone who is involved with terrorism and is attempting to enter Great Britain or Northern Ireland for terrorist purposes. Exclusion orders under this section cannot be made against British citizens.

Schedule 2 of the PTA provides that exclusion orders can be revoked at any time by the Secretary of State, and must expire at the end of three years. Successive exclusion orders are permitted.

People who are excluded have no right to hear the evidence, to cross-examine witnesses, to present a defense, or to be represented by counsel. Furthermore, those excluded cannot challenge the decision in court--all they can do is to make a "representation" to the Secretary of State within seven days, stating grounds for an objection to the exclusion order (Schedule 2(3)). The representation must be in writing; the target of the order can also request a personal interview with someone appointed by the Secretary of State. A person trying to avoid exclusion bears the burden of proof (Schedule 2 (9)(1)).

Senior lawyers in private practice act as advisors to the Home Secretary in cases in which excluded persons make representations to the Home Secretary. These advisors look at the Home Office's papers and interview the police who have asked for exclusion, as well as the excluded person and his or her attorney, if represented. According to the Home Office, orders to exclude have on occasion been reversed, but most are not; the Home Secretary reportedly personally examines each case and usually takes the recommendation of the independent advisor.

A person may be detained between the time an exclusion order is issued and directions are given for his or her removal from the country. A person who is on a ship or an airplane may be prevented from disembarking and held in custody; a person may be removed from an automobile and detained (Schedule 2 (7)).

According to the US State Department's 1990 Country Report on Human Rights in the UK, in the period between November 1978 and September 1990, orders of exclusion were issued for 293 people. At present, according to the Home Office in London, about 100 exclusion orders are in effect. Ninety-five of these exclude people from Great Britain or the UK as a whole; five or six orders exclude people from Northern Ireland.

The consequences for a person who is excluded are extremely serious. Exclusion can mean loss of a job, loss of a place to live, loss of contact with family and friends. It can also be dangerous, since an excluded person will be stigmatized as someone involved with terrorism, and thus a possible target for opposing paramilitaries.

The procedure in exclusion cases is also subject to abuse. For example, suspects can be detained under the PTA for as long as seven days. If served with an exclusion order at the end of that time, they can be detained for another seven days, unless they agree to be sent out of the country. If an individual exercises the right to make a representation to the Secretary of State, detention can be extended until the Secretary of State makes a decision. The Secretary of State is required to make a decision "as soon as is reasonably practicable," but no time limit is set.[119]

The government has justified exclusion orders as a necessary means of deterring terrorism. One government spokesperson told the Helsinki Watch mission that exclusion orders are justified by the government as a "valuable means of disrupting terrorist activity." Some cases allegedly involve people who are procuring arms in Great Britain for use by paramilitaries in Northern Ireland. The spokesperson said that there are cases in which intelligence sources cannot be revealed; instead of charging and trying these individuals, they are simply excluded from either Northern Ireland or Great Britain. Another spokesperson for the Northern Ireland Office told the Helsinki Watch mission that

---

[119] See *Justice Under Fire: The Abuse of Civil Liberties in Northern Ireland*. Anthony Jennings, Ed. London, Pluto Press, 1990. P. 167.

"decisions are sometimes made on the basis of information that, if revealed, would put lives at risk. Normality is not always possible in a situation of terrorism."

International Freedom of Movement Standards

The right to freedom of movement has been spelled out in various international declarations and agreements. Article 9 of the Universal Declaration of Human Rights, for example, states that no one shall be subjected to arbitrary arrest, detention or exile. Article 13 provides:

> 1. Everyone has the right to freedom of movement and residence within the borders of each State.
>
> 2. Everyone has the right to leave a country, including his own, and to return to his country.

Article 12 (1) of the International Covenant on Civil and Political Rights (ICCPR) states that "[e]veryone lawfully within the territory of a State shall, within that territory, have the right to liberty of movement and freedom to choose his residence." Article 12 (3) provides that this right may be restricted for reasons of "national security, public order, public health or morals or the rights and freedoms of others." The Fourth Protocol to the European Convention on Human Rights contains similar guarantees.[120]

---

[120] The Fourth Protocol to the European Convention on Human Rights also guarantees liberty of movement and freedom to choose a residence to people lawfully within a State's territory. That right is also subject to restrictions based on national security or public order (Article 2). The United Kingdom has signed and ratified the European Convention on Human Rights, but not Protocol Four.

Article 12(4) of the International Covenant on Civil and Political Rights states that "[n]o one shall be arbitrarily deprived of the right to enter his own country."[121]

With regard to detention, ICCPR Article 9 (4) states:

Anyone who is deprived of his liberty by arrest or detention shall be entitled to take proceedings before a

---

[121] Article 3 of Protocol Four to the European Convention on Human Rights also provides that "[n]o one shall be deprived of the right to enter the territory of the State of which he is a national." The same article states that "[n]o one shall be expelled, by means either of an individual or of a collective measure, from the territory of the State of which he is a national."

The January 1989 Concluding Document of the Vienna Follow-up Meeting of the Commission on Security and Cooperation in Europe (CSCE) (The Helsinki Final Act) provides that

[t]he participating States [including the UK] will respect fully the right of everyone to freedom of movement and residence within the borders of each State, and to leave any country, including his own, and to return to his country (Principle 19). . . [and] ensure that no one shall be subjected to arbitrary arrest, detention or exile (Principle 23a).

The June 1990 Document of the Copenhagen Meeting of the Conference on the Human Dimension of the CSCE says that participating States (including the UK) reaffirm that

they will respect the right of everyone to leave any country, including his own, and to return to his country, consistent with a State's international obligations and CSCE commitments. Restrictions on this right will have the character of very rare exceptions, will be considered necessary only if they respond to a specific public need, pursue a legitimate aim and are proportionate to that aim, and will not be abused or applied in an arbitrary manner (Principle 9.5).

court, in order that the court may decide without delay on the lawfulness of his detention and order his release if the detention is not lawful.

Article 10 of the Universal Declaration of Human Rights says:

Everyone is entitled in full equality to a fair and public hearing by an independent and impartial tribunal, in the determination of his *rights and obligations* and of any criminal charge against him [emphasis added].

The European Convention on Human Rights says in Article 6 (1):

In the determination of his *civil rights and obligations* or of any criminal charge against him, everyone is entitled to a fair and public hearing within a reasonable time by an independent and impartial tribunal established by law... [emphasis added].

The Vienna Concluding Document to the CSCE contains similar guarantees.[122]

---

[122]Principle 13(i) of the Vienna Concluding Document states that participating States shall

ensure that effective remedies as well as full information about them are available to those who claim that their human rights and fundamental freedoms have been violated; they will, *inter alia*, effectively apply the following remedies:

* the right of the individual to appeal to executive, legislative, judicial or administrative organs;

* the right to a fair and public hearing within a reasonable time before an independent and impartial tribunal, including the right to present legal arguments and to be represented by legal counsel of one's choice;

* the right to be promptly and officially informed of the decision taken on any appeal, including the legal grounds on

*   *   *

The Helsinki Watch mission concluded that excluding suspects pursuant to the exclusion orders provided in the Prevention of Terrorism Act is a form of internal exile and an unjustified deprivation of due process of law. Suspects have to answer unknown charges, defend against unknown evidence and persuade the Secretary of State of their innocence. The exclusion power provides the government with a means of avoiding the criminal justice system and allows the infliction of punishment with no procedural safeguards. Indeed, there have been occasions on which a defendant has been found not guilty of an offense connected with political violence, only to be served with an exclusion order on leaving the courthouse.

> * A Loyalist told the Helsinki Watch mission that he had been arrested in Liverpool in 1986 and held for seven days, then charged with conspiracy to import guns from Canada. He was held for three months without bail; then the charges were dropped on May 19, 1986. He was then served with an exclusion order, which was subsequently renewed. As a result, he cannot go to London; as a practical matter, it is difficult for him to go to the continent, as he can't go through London, and there is only one flight from Belfast to Amsterdam. When he made a representation to the Home Office to reverse his exclusion, he was told, "You tell us why you shouldn't be excluded."

The Helsinki Watch mission met with others who had been subjected to exclusion orders:

> * A Nationalist in his twenties who lives in a Republican area in East Belfast told the Helsinki Watch mission that

---

> which this decision was based. This information will be provided as a rule in writing and, in any event, in a way that will enable the individual to make effective use of further available remedies.

123

he had been arrested in May 1990 under Section 14 of the PTA after getting off a boat in Scotland. An inspector in uniform asked him the purpose of his visit and where he was staying. He was searched, photographed, fingerprinted and put into a cell. He was held for 48 hours and then was told he would be held for an additional 48 hours. At the end of that time, he was told that an exclusion order was coming from London. He was held for a further 14 hours and then served with an order excluding him from all of the UK (except Northern Ireland). Although he was never asked any questions about terrorist activity during his detention, he was told that the exclusion order was based on his instigating or participating in acts of terrorism.

Helsinki Watch recommends that exclusion orders be abolished, and that people suspected of acts of political violence be tried lawfully in courts in Great Britain or in Northern Ireland.

The exclusionary power is enormously far-reaching in its impact on individuals and is conducted without a semblance of fair procedure, as the Standing Advisory Commission on Human Rights has stated to support its recommendation that the PTA's exclusion powers be repealed:

> The power to exclude persons under the Act is the most exceptional of the emergency powers conferred by the legislation and [SACHR] recommends that [these sections] should not be reenacted in any future Act and should be allowed to lapse when Parliament next considers their renewal. The continuation of a power which grants such wide discretion to the Secretary of State requires the most exceptional circumstances and unambiguous evidence of the threat posed to national security or public order or the rights or freedoms of others. The evidence of that threat is not apparent to [SACHR] especially when it considers the powers available to the police under the ordinary criminal law. The procedure does not lend itself to openness or perceived fairness and given the nature of the power to exclude, the lack of proof of its utility in the fight against

124

terrorism and its punitive effect as a power of internal exile, [SACHR] strongly recommends that the power to remove persons from one part of the United Kingdom to another must be repealed.[123]

John Alderdice, the leader of the Alliance party, told the Helsinki Watch mission that Northern Ireland is part of the UK, and that he sees no argument in favor of retaining the power to issue orders of exclusion. Tom Lyne, a spokesperson for M.P. Kevin McNamara, and the British Labor Party's researcher on Northern Ireland, told Helsinki Watch that the Labor Party opposes exclusion orders. "They are outrageous," he said, "particularly when people are excluded right after they've been acquitted in court."

---

[123] Standing Advisory Commission on Human Rights, *13th Report for 1986-87*, p. 58.

VIII. FREEDOM OF EXPRESSION

The Broadcasting Ban

On October 19, 1988, then-Home Secretary Douglas Hurd sent to the British Broadcasting Corporation (BBC) and the Independent Broadcasting Authority (IBA) notices requesting that they refrain at all times from broadcasting

> any words spoken whether in the course of an interview or discussion or otherwise, by a person who appears or is heard on the programme in which the matter is broadcast where

> (a) the person speaking the words represents or purports to represent an organisation specified in paragraph 2 below, or

> (b) the words support or solicit or invite support for such an organisation.[124]

This order, subsequently known as the "Broadcasting Ban," or the "Media Ban," was issued under Section 29 of the Broadcasting Act of 1981 and the BBC's Charter.

The eleven organizations specified in paragraph 2 included banned Republican paramilitary groups (the IRA, its women's and youth wings, the INLA (Irish National Liberation Army) and Saor Eire; illegal Loyalist paramilitary groups (the Ulster Volunteer Force (UVF), the Ulster Freedom Fighters (UFF) and the Red Hand Commandos); a legal Loyalist paramilitary group, the Ulster Defense Association (UDA); and two legal political parties--Sinn Fein, the political arm of the IRA, and a smaller group, Republican Sinn Fein.[125]

---

[124] *Speak No Evil: The British Broadcasting Ban, The Media and the Conflict in Ireland.* Glasgow University Media Group. Glasgow, 1990, page 14.

[125] *No Comment: Censorship, Secrecy and the Irish Troubles.* Article 19, London,

Under the ban a person's face can be seen on television; the words the person speaks can be read by someone else, paraphrased, or printed on the screen, but the individual's own voice cannot be heard. In guidelines drawn up by the Home Office, two exceptions to the ban are permitted: (1) members of the banned organizations are allowed to speak on radio or TV during election campaigns or during proceedings at Parliament in Westminster, and (2) elected representatives--Sinn Fein councillors and Member of Parliament Gerry Adams--are allowed to be heard speaking about constituency matters, as long as they are not speaking on behalf of an organization listed in the ban. (Commentators promptly pointed out that in some situations it is difficult, if not impossible, to determine whether an elected official, when discussing issues concerning constituents, is speaking as well for an organization.)

According to Home Secretary Hurd, the Broadcasting Ban was initiated because the appearance on radio or TV of members of paramilitary groups had "caused widespread offense" to listeners and viewers.[126] Prime Minister Margaret Thatcher said of the ban, "To beat off your enemy in a war, you have to suspend some of your civil liberties for a time."[127]

A spokesperson for the Northern Ireland Office told Helsinki Watch that the Broadcasting Ban is not censorship, since a person's views can be heard--it is only his voice that is kept off the air. He reported that the government believes that a person's appearance on television is an "emotional layer" on top of the words, and that the appearance of "terrorists" on television caused an "intolerable level of offense."[128]

1989, page 24.

[126] *No Comment, op cit.*, page 26.

[127] *Ibid.*, page 25.

[128] This has led to absurd situations like a December 1990 interview with Gerry Adams in which an actor's reading of Adams's words was synchronized with Adams's appearance on television; unless viewers knew Adams's voice, they would have thought Adams himself was speaking.

127

A spokesperson for the Home Office in London told the Helsinki Watch mission that the ban had been set up because television and radio appearances by persons associated with terrorist organizations "caused offense to ordinary, law-abiding members of the public; because [the media presented] a platform for publicity for paramilitaries, and lent them a spurious respectability; and because it was used to intimidate law-abiding people in Northern Ireland--if someone was killed because he or she worked for or supported security forces, a paramilitary supporter would say, 'he was killed because he supported security forces--let this be a warning.' In other words, the government introduced the measure to protect the public from intimidation." The spokesperson asserted that the fact that the number of inquiries of Sinn Fein by journalists had declined considerably indicated that the ban had been effective.

Article 19, the London-based freedom of expression group, reports that voice-overs of Sinn Fein speakers were used thirty times by the BBC during the first year of the ban's existence.[129] Most of these voice-overs were used in current news reports, but many others related to historical or archival material.

Some of the programs affected were:

* A children's history series, *Understanding Northern Ireland*, which was not allowed to show Ireland's first Prime Minister, Eamonn de Valera, or Nobel Peace Prize winner and former IRA chief of staff, Sean McBride.[130]

* The film *Mother Ireland*, which included an interview with Mairead Farrell, who was shot and killed by security forces in Gibraltar in 1988, was rejected by Channel 4.

* The song, "Streets of Sorrow/Birmingham Six," which was banned by the IBA in November 1988. Performed by the group The Pogues, the song proclaims the

---

[129] *Ibid.*, page 32.

[130] *Index on Censorship*, October 1990, page 34.

innocence of the Guildford Four and the Birmingham Six (all subsequently released by the British government as miscarriages of justice). The IBA banned the song because it "solicited or invited support" for a listed organization because it contained a "general disagreement with the way in which the British government responds to and the courts deal with the terrorist threat in the UK."[131]

* The Thames TV series, *The Troubles,* which first appeared in 1981, had to be re-edited before it could be shown again in 1989.[132]

* A passage in a Channel 4 film, "Trouble the Calm," which was cut out and subtitled in May 1989. A caption read: "Under government broadcasting restrictions, in force since October 1988, this woman cannot explain her husband's beliefs and motivations which led to his imprisonment."[133]

The Broadcasting Ban has also resulted in self-censorship because of difficulties in interpreting the ban. Deciding whether someone who is not a member of a listed organization will speak in "support" of a listed organization or will "solicit or invite support for such an organization" is not always easy. A broadcaster must either pre-record an interview and expurgate prohibited words, or play it safe and refrain from interviews. A number of people who are not members of listed organizations have been banned, including Brighton Labour Councillor Richard Stanton, former M.P. Bernadette Devlin McAliskey, American author Margie Bernard, and an uncle of Paul Hill, one of the "Guildford Four."[134]

---

[131] *The Observer,* Nov. 20, 1988. Quoted in *Speak No Evil, op. cit.,* p. 47.

[132] *No Comment, op. cit.,* pages 32 and 33.

[133] News release for *Speak No Evil,* October 11, 1990, page 2.

[134] *Ibid.*

Elected representatives, including Hugh Brady, a Sinn Fein councilor in London/Derry, told the Helsinki Watch mission that although Sinn Fein councillors are supposed to be able to speak about social and economic issues--issues of direct concern to their constituents--as long as they are not speaking on behalf of a listed organization, they are frequently denied the opportunity to appear on radio or television. Hugh Brady told us that the Broadcasting Ban has affected him directly. "Not every councillor can speak on radio or TV," he said; "you can only talk if you are the chair of a major committee. Also, when an actor reads your words, they can be misconstrued." On the other hand, a spokesperson for the banned Loyalist group, the Ulster Defense Association, told Helsinki Watch that the Broadcasting Ban had not significantly affected the UDA.

On December 19, 1990, Home Secretary Kenneth Baker announced that the Broadcasting Ban would continue, and would be extended to include for the first time cable and non-domestic satellite television services. Explaining the extension, Secretary Baker said:

> The Government believes the current broadcasting restrictions have proved effective in generally preventing terrorist spokesmen and their supporters from gaining direct access to television and radio in this country, and thus denying them the publicity they continually seek.[135]

John Alderdice, leader of the Alliance Party, told the Helsinki Watch mission that the government's approach, as reflected in the Broadcasting Ban, is "incoherent and nonsensical. I sit on the Belfast City Council; Sinn Fein is there too, but they can't be interviewed on the issues and broadcast." Tom Lyne, the British Labor Party's researcher on Northern Ireland, told the mission that the Labor Party opposes the ban.

---

[135] *The Guardian*, December 12, 1990.

International Freedom of Expression Standards

Freedom of expression is guaranteed by international agreements. Article 19 of the International Covenant on Civil and Political Rights states:

1. Everyone shall have the right to hold opinions without interference.

2. Everyone shall have the right to freedom of expression; this right shall include freedom to seek, receive and impart information and ideas of all kinds, regardless of frontiers, either orally, in writing or in print, in the form of art, or through any other media of his choice.

3. The exercise of the rights provided for in paragraph 2 of this article carries with it special duties and responsibilities. It may therefore be subject to certain restrictions, but these shall only be such as are provided by law and are necessary:

 (a) For respect of the rights or reputations of others;
 (b) For the protection of national security or of public order (*ordre public*), or of public health or morals.

Article 10 of the European Convention for the Protection of Human Rights and Fundamental Freedoms states:

1. Everyone has the right to freedom of expression. This right shall include freedom to hold opinions and to receive and impart information and ideas without interference by public authority and regardless of frontiers. This Article shall not prevent States from requiring the licensing of broadcasting, television or cinema enterprises.

131

2. The exercise of these freedoms, since it carries with it duties and responsibilities, may be subject to such formalities, conditions, restrictions or penalties as are prescribed by law and are necessary in a democratic society, in the interests of national security, territorial integrity or public safety, for the prevention of disorder or crime, for the protection of health or morals, for the protection of the reputation or rights of others, for preventing the disclosure of information received in confidence, or for maintaining the authority and impartiality of the judiciary.

Both of these international agreements provide for freedom of expression, subject only to significant national security, public order or public safety interests. The Home Secretary did not base the media ban on the need for national security, public order, or any of the other factors set forth in the ICCPR and the European Human Rights Convention. Rather, he said that the appearance on radio or TV of supporters of paramilitary groups had "caused widespread offense" to listeners or viewers. To our knowledge, no one has asserted that the Broadcasting Ban was necessary for the protection of national security or public order.

Helsinki Watch believes that the Broadcasting Ban should be revoked. Exchanges of views and open debate are essential in a democracy. To deny advocates of a particular political viewpoint the opportunity to state their case directly is to deny others the opportunity to debate them, and to deny citizens the information they need to make informed decisions essential to the functioning of a democratic society. It is well established that censorship and secrecy work against the democratic process. Governments should not determine whose views will be heard; in a free society, the freedom to receive, as well as to impart, information is crucial. Freedom of speech should never be restricted on the basis of its subject matter or the identity of the speaker; curbs must be based on a direct and immediate relationship to imminent violence. The Broadcasting Ban fails each of these tests.

Harassment of the Media by Paramilitaries and Security Forces

There is reliable information that journalists are frequently intimidated by both paramilitary groups and security forces. For example, Article 19 reported a 1988 kidnapping of a journalist by the IRA, who questioned him about his sources. Article 19 also reported a case in which a national TV journalist was threatened by the Ulster Defense Association, a Loyalist paramilitary group, because of a documentary on racketeering on which he was working.[136]

Under the EPA, police can seize photographers' film or photographs without a court order. A free-lance reporter in Omagh told the Helsinki Watch mission:

> A year or so ago I started taking pictures of RUC officers attacking two young women; one girl was dragged from a car and another was attacked inside the car. When the RUC saw me, one yelled, "Get the bastard." Four of them went after me, hitting me. They took my camera with the film.

Paramilitaries, too, have been reported to seize film and cameras.

The UK and the NIO should ensure that freedom of expression is protected in Northern Ireland by making every effort to safeguard journalists from attacks by paramilitary groups, and by appropriately disciplining security force members who harass or abuse members of the press who are performing their professional duties.

---

[136] *Freedom of Expression and Information in the United Kingdom*, Article 19, London, March 1991, page 25.

Political Vetting of Community Organizations

At least 26 organizations have lost funding since 1985 because the Northern Ireland Office decided that they had "sufficiently close links to paramilitary organizations."[137] An organization is not told the reasons for this action, is not given a hearing or an opportunity to state its own case or to cross-examine witnesses against it.

Political vetting in Northern Ireland began on June 27, 1985, when then-Secretary of State for Northern Ireland Douglas Hurd reported to Parliament that, while the government was determined to support genuine "voluntary and community-based activity" in Northern Ireland,

> I am satisfied, from information available to me, that there are cases in which some community groups, or persons prominent in the direction or management of some community groups, have sufficiently close links with paramilitary organisations to give rise to a grave risk that to give support to those groups would have the effect of improving the standing and furthering the aims of a paramilitary organisation, whether directly or indirectly. I do not consider that any such use of government funds would be in the public interest, and in any particular case in which I am satisfied that these conditions prevail no grant will be paid.[138]

On the same day, a letter was sent to the Conway Mill Women's Self-Help Group in West Belfast from the Department of Economic Development (DED), stating that the Secretary of State had decided it was not in the public interest to continue the group's DED grant. No reason was given for taking away the funding.

---

[137] Statement of Northern Ireland Office, reported on the BBC in September 1990.

[138] *The Political Vetting of Community Work in Northern Ireland*, The Political Vetting of Community Work Working Group, Belfast, October 1990, page 3.

Since that time, a number of other groups have fallen victim to such "political vetting," as it came to be called. Among them are:

> * Conway Community Enterprises, a group that organized small job creation units, lost funding for four Action for Community Employment (ACE) workers in 1985.

> * Conway Mill Creche lost funding for two ACE workers in 1985.

> * Conway Education Centre, an adjunct of community education work carried out by Springhill Community House, lost money in 1985 for tutors who were working in Conway Mill.[139]

> * La, an Irish language daily newspaper based in Conway Mill, lost funding for five ACE workers in September 1985.

> * Shantallow Tenants' Association's application for funding for eleven ACE workers was denied, and its existing workers terminated in February 1986.

> * Dove House, London/Derry, lost four ACE workers in June 1986, but lobbied successfully for reinstatement in August 1986.

> * Naiscoil Mhic Airt, an Irish language nursery school in Belfast, lost funding for five ACE workers in 1987.

> * Twinbrook Tenants' and Community Association lost six ACE workers in August 1987.

---

[139] Conway Mill, an old flax mill in Conway Street off the Falls road, closed in 1974. In 1982, a group of community people leased the empty building to encourage economic development in West Belfast and to promote education. *Ibid.*, page 13.

* Glencairn Community Association lost funding for 53 ACE workers in December 1989.[140]

* Belfast Exposed, a photography association, received funding for one ACE worker in 1984, a year before Secretary Hurd's statement, on condition that the worker be based anywhere but at Conway Mill.

In none of these cases was an organization given an explanation for its loss of funding.[141]

In the most recent case, an Irish language group, Glor na nGael, was deprived of its funding in August 1990. Glor na nGael (the voice or language of the Gael), an all-Ireland Irish language competition set up in 1961, was organized in West Belfast in 1982, at the time of a revival of interest in the Irish language. The Belfast group has worked to set up Irish street signs, and to encourage Irish language education. In recent years, the group has organized and provided services for seven of the eight Irish nursery schools in Belfast; it has provided classes in the Irish language for the Protestant, as well as for the Catholic community; and it has trained people in the teaching of a second language. The group has won awards, including an All-Ireland Prize for doing the most for the Irish language, and has been widely praised.

Glor na nGael's ACE funding began in 1984. Its 1990 budget came largely from a 90,000 pound annual grant from the government's Training and Employment Agency for ACE workers. The group used the ACE funding to train twenty long-term unemployed people.

---

[140] *Ibid.*, pages 4 and 5.

[141] The NIO has the power to dispense outside funds, as well as its own. The European Community, through the European Social Fund and the European Regional Development Fund, for example, provided nearly 197 million pounds to the Department of Economic Development (DED) between 1982 and 1987. Most of this money went to ACE and Youth Training Programs (YTP). Also, money from the International Fund for Ireland, most of which comes from the United States Government, is funneled through the NIO.

On August 25, 1990, Glor na nGael received a letter from the Training and Employment Agency telling the staff that the funding would end on August 31, 1990. The letter gave no reason for the decision except to say that it was based on the policy laid out in Douglas Hurd's 1985 statement.

Noirin Ui Chleirigh, the group's chairperson, told the Helsinki Watch mission in January 1991: "We believe that language is not political. Learning the Irish language has led our people to have greater self-respect and self-worth. It shows us that we are not stupid. Underneath everything else in Belfast, there is a feeling of no hope--unemployment is very high, and all people can do is think of ways to diddle money out of the dole. Some people get in a rut and don't even apply for jobs any more because they have been turned down so often. Glor na nGael had a ripple effect--a feeling of pride that we could do something on our own. We've had success rehabilitating people--four of our people have gone on to university."

Ms. Ui Chleirigh told us that she herself had felt inferior--like a second-class citizen. "One of my kids has been educated in English, and two in Irish. The two who've been educated in Irish have more self-respect and self-confidence; they're not defensive about being Irish. The Irish language can be a great unifying force."

William Smith, the Unionist who heads Justice for All, an organization devoted to exposing government harassment of the Protestant community, told the Helsinki Watch mission:

> One of the biggest cases of political vetting happened here. Fifty-three people lost their jobs at the Glencairn Community Association. The government just walked in and said, "We're closing you down." There was no time to argue. They thought a couple of the members were paramilitaries, so the whole community was "linked to paramilitaries." And political vetting can extend into your social life--to hold office in a social club, like a snooker club, you have to get a licence every year, and the officers' names are listed. Police will oppose your licence if they suspect anyone of connections with paramilitaries. It happened to three clubs this week--

people had to get off the list of officers because they had served time. In one case, someone served five years fifteen years ago; another served three years twelve years ago.

Political vetting can seriously harm a community group, not only in denying funding, but in branding the group as being close to a paramilitary organization. Membership declines if people are afraid to be associated with a vetted group, fearing that they will be tarred as "having close links to paramilitary organizations." Such allegations also raise the possibility that a vetted group may be targeted for violence-- even political assassination--by opposing paramilitaries. Some groups have reported that their effectiveness has been sharply curtailed. Targeted groups have reported difficulties in raising money from other sources once they have been marked as having close links to paramilitaries. Political vetting has effectively meant blacklisting organizations. And, inevitably, it has also resulted in self-censorship--a sort of self-vetting--in which groups try to avoid any actions that might be construed by the government as suggesting ties to paramilitary groups.[142]

Helsinki Watch believes that the Northern Ireland Office should demonstrate a reasonable basis for a decision to remove funding from a community organization, should explain its reasons, and should not deny funding on political grounds. In addition, we believe that a group that is about to be denied funding should be given the right to an impartial hearing, including an opportunity to learn the specific charges against it, to present its case, and to cross-examine opposing witnesses. If the government has evidence of illegal activity on the part of community groups or individuals associated with them, it should pursue this through the courts.

Although the NIO is not required to fund all community groups, a grant process should be impartial and non-partisan. Voluntary associations should be able to operate independently and without

---

[142] For a full discussion of the effect of political vetting on community groups in Northern Ireland, see *The Political Vetting of Community Work in Northern Ireland, op cit.*

interference by the government. The government's current practice of removing funding for what appear to be political reasons threatens freedom of expression and freedom of association.

Non-Violence Declarations Required for Councillors

Anyone who runs for a seat on a district council in Northern Ireland is required by the Elected Authorities (Northern Ireland) Act 1988 to sign a declaration stating:

> If elected, I will not by word or deed express support for or approval of
>
> > a) any proscribed organization or
> > b) acts of terrorism (that is to say, violence for political ends) connected with the affairs of Northern Ireland.

Since the enactment of this law, Sinn Fein candidates for council seats have all signed the declaration. Republican Sinn Fein, a smaller group, announced that its candidates would not sign such a declaration.

Historically, loyalty oaths have been used in many countries as a weapon against individual rights. Helsinki Watch believes that the requirement for councillors to sign declarations repudiating proscribed organizations or the use of violence for political ends violates the right to freedom of expression and should be abolished. The Standing Advisory Commission on Human Rights opposed the oaths, and stated that it is:

> fundamentally wrong [to] devise artificial means to exclude councillors from local politics; such policies cannot hope to succeed in the long term.[143]

---

[143] *No Comment: Censorship, Secrecy and the Irish Troubles.* Article 19, London, 1989, p.76.

IX. TRANSFER OF PRISONERS

A number of prisoners from Northern Ireland are serving sentences in prisons in Great Britain. The prisoners, their families, and several organizations concerned with the criminal justice system and the treatment of offenders, advocate transferring these prisoners to prisons in Northern Ireland.

For families of prisoners, incarceration of prisoners in England has created many serious problems. First, it is difficult, time-consuming and expensive to travel to Britain to visit a prisoner. The sister of one prisoner told the Helsinki Watch mission that her brother had been at one time imprisoned on the Isle of Wight; it took 23 hours to get to the prison by train, bus and ferry, at a cost of 250 to 300 pounds per person. The family was able to visit only once or twice a year.

Visiting is especially difficult for mothers with small children. One woman told us that her husband had been in eight different prisons in seven years. She sees him four or five times a year; no conjugal visits are allowed. At Easter and during the summer, she tries to take their children along; the children see their father only for about twenty hours a year. "Their daddy has become a fantasy," she said. "The children don't know him at all."

For people living on government assistance, insufficient money is allotted for travel expenses to overseas prisons, and overnight accommodations are often inadequate and expensive. At times, families arrive in England after an arduous journey only to be told that the prisoner has just been transferred to another prison, frequently at a great distance. Also, families complain of harassment by police at ports when leaving or entering Northern Ireland, because they are relatives of prisoners.

The Helsinki Watch mission met with the Committee for the Transfer of Irish Prisoners. Members of the Committee said that there are approximately 40 Republican prisoners in British prisons; all want to be transferred to Northern Ireland. The Committee reported that the British government gives various reasons for not transferring the

140

prisoners: returned prisoners could be security risks, or could disrupt prison life in local prisons; their crimes "offended common decency."

The Committee believes that the families of the prisoners are victimized. One member said:

> The bulk of the relatives are working class women, who either earn low incomes or receive benefits from the state. Lots of young children and elderly relatives are involved. For financial and physical reasons it's very hard to travel long distances.

The Committee reports that prisoners convicted of ordinary crimes can, after some lobbying by interested groups, secure transfers to Northern Ireland from Britain, but that those convicted of politically-motivated crimes cannot.

A prisoner in England may apply for transfer to a prison in Northern Ireland, but under Section 26(1) of the 1961 Criminal Justice Act the decision is discretionary.

In response to a question concerning the basis on which the government considers requests by prisoners for transfers, Home Secretary Douglas Hurd said on June 23, 1989:

> Any inmate in England and Wales, Scotland or Northern Ireland who applies to be transferred to either of the other jurisdictions to serve the rest of his or her sentence will normally be transferred, provided that
>
> (1) the inmate would have at least six months left to serve in the receiving jurisdiction before his or her date of release;
>
> (2) the inmate was ordinarily resident in the receiving jurisdiction prior to the current sentence; or his or her close family currently reside there and there are reasonable grounds for believing that it is the inmate's firm intention to take up residence there on release; and

(3) both Departments concerned are reasonably satisfied that the inmate will not, if transferred, disrupt or attempt to disrupt any prison establishment, or otherwise pose an unacceptable risk to security.

Even if these conditions are met, however, transfer may be refused it it is considered that the inmate's crimes were so serious as to render him or her undeserving of any degree of public sympathy or to make it inappropriate that the inmate should benefit from a substantial reduction in time left to serve, if that would be a consequence of transfer. Similarly, transfers may be refused if there are reasonable grounds for believing that the inmate's primary intention in making the application is to secure a reduction in the time left to serve. On the other hand, an application that does not meet these conditions may nevertheless be granted where there are strong compassionate or other compelling grounds for transfer.

Principle 20 of the United Nations' "Body of Principles for the Protection of all Persons Under Any Form of Detention or Imprisonment" states:

If a detained or imprisoned person so requests, he shall if possible be kept in a place of detention or imprisonment reasonably near his usual place of residence.

Helsinki Watch believes that the UK should, on humanitarian grounds, and in keeping with international standards, make every effort to transfer to Northern Ireland prisoners who wish to be transferred. For those whose transfers are denied, the UK should make public its reasons for refusing the transfer.

X. RECOMMENDATIONS

Helsinki Watch makes the following recommendations to the government of the United Kingdom:

Arrest, Search, Detention and Interrogation

* Detainees should have immediate and regular access to attorneys.

* Detainees should be brought before a court within 48 hours of detention.

* The UK should repeal its derogation from Article 5(3) of the European Convention on Human Rights.

* The RUC should prevent abuse of detainees during interrogations and appropriately discipline officers who carry out such abuse.

* All interrogations should be video- and audiotaped with strict regulations against unwarranted disclosure.

* Detainees' attorneys should have access to all video- and audio-tapes of interrogations.

* The power to intern suspects without judicial authorization should be abolished.

* The UK should take steps to end random street stops and searches and to ensure that all searches are conducted without degrading or harassing measures.

* The EPA's search and entry powers should be repealed.

* A warrant should be required for examining or seizing documents.

Use of Lethal Force by Security Forces

* The UK should enact legislation and issue guidelines that strictly control the use of force in Northern Ireland. The standard for the use of lethal force by security forces should be "absolute necessity"; the force used should be in proportion to the actual danger.

* The use of the plastic bullet in Northern Ireland should be banned.

Investigation of the Use of Lethal Force by Security Forces

* Offenses of "manslaughter" and "unreasonable or excessive use of force" should be added to the Northern Ireland Criminal Code for cases involving the use of lethal force by security forces.

* Complaints against security force personnel should be promptly and thoroughly investigated by an independent organization with subpoena power and adequate trained investigatory staff.

* The United Kingdom should follow the United Nations Economic and Social Council's "Principles on the Effective Prevention and Investigation of Extra-Legal, Arbitrary and Summary Executions" in cases of killings by security forces, including:

> A thorough, prompt and impartial investigation of all suspected cases of extra-legal, arbitrary and summary executions;

> Power in the investigative authority to obtain all information necessary to the inquiry; authority to oblige witnesses and officials allegedly involved in any such executions to appear and testify, and to demand the production of evidence;

> An independent commission of inquiry for those cases in which the established investigative procedures are inadequate because of lack of expertise or impartiality, and for cases where there are complaints from the family of the victim about these inadequacies or other substantial reasons;

144

An adequate autopsy conducted by an impartial and independent physician who is an expert in forensic pathology and is given access to all investigative data;

Protection from violence or intimidation for complainants, witnesses, families and investigators;

Removal from power or control over complainants, witnesses, families or investigators of anyone potentially implicated in extra-legal, summary or arbitrary executions;

Access by families and their legal representatives to any hearing and to all relevant information, and the right to present other evidence;

Right of a family to have a representative present at the autopsy;

A detailed written report on the methods and findings of the investigation to be made public within a reasonable time;

A government response to the report of the investigation within a reasonable time, either replying to the report or indicating the steps to be taken in response to it;

Government action to bring to justice persons identified by the investigation as having taken part in extra-legal, arbitrary and summary executions;

No right to claim an order from a superior officer or a public authority as justification for extra-legal, summary or arbitrary execution;

Responsibility of superiors, officers or other public officials for acts committed under their authority if they had a reasonable opportunity to prevent such acts; no blanket immunity from prosecution to any person involved in such acts; and

Fair and adequate compensation for the families and dependents of victims of extra-legal, arbitrary and summary executions within a reasonable period of time.

* The Coroners' Law and Rules for Northern Ireland should, at a minimum, be brought into line with the law and rules for England and Wales:

In cases in which criminal charges may be brought against a suspect, the coroner's inquest should be adjourned for a specific period of time; if at the end of that time the DPP has not decided whether to prosecute, the inquest should be resumed.

Coroners' juries should have the power to reach a full verdict, such as "unlawful killing by unnamed persons."

Persons who are suspected of causing the death at issue should be compelled to testify in person, but should not be required to answer questions that might incriminate themselves.

Families of victims killed by security forces should be eligible for legal aid assistance so that they can be aided before and during the inquest by an attorney.

Families of victims and their representatives should have access to autopsy reports, documents, witnesses' statements and other evidence to be introduced at an inquest, and adequate time to prepare for the inquest after receiving this information.

The Right to a Fair Trial

* Jury trials should gradually be resumed for "scheduled offenses" in Northern Ireland; steps should be taken to prevent the intimidation of witnesses and jurors.

* The number of "scheduled offenses" should be reduced.

* The attorney general should be required to "schedule in" cases in which political violence played a part, rather than "scheduling out" cases in which political violence played no part.

* Defendants should have the right to waive jury trials.

* The EPA standard for the admissibility of confessions should be abolished.

* The Criminal Evidence (NI) Order, which permits a court to draw adverse inferences from a suspect's refusal to answer questions asked by police during interrogation or at trial, should be rescinded.

* Special efforts should be made to protect lawyers who represent defendants in political terrorism cases to guarantee that they can represent clients without interference, harassment or intimidation. Harassment of lawyers should be investigated and appropriately punished.

Freedom of Movement

* The PTA orders of exclusion should be abolished.

Freedom of Expression

* The Broadcasting Ban should be abolished.

* The UK and the Northern Ireland Office should make every effort to safeguard journalists from attacks by paramilitary groups, and should appropriately discipline security force members who harass or abuse members of the press.

* The requirement that councillors sign declarations repudiating proscribed organizations or the use of violence for political ends should be abolished.

* The Northern Ireland Office should not deny funding to community organizations on political grounds. The NIO should demonstrate a reasonable basis for a decision to remove funding for community organizations, and should make public its reasons. A group that is to be denied funding should have the right to an impartial hearing.

Transfer of Prisoners

* The UK should make every effort to transfer to Northern Ireland prisoners who wish to be transferred.

* * *

With regard to the use of force by paramilitary groups, Helsinki Watch recommends that such groups refrain from violating the basic principles that underlie international humanitarian law by the use of lethal force, the taking of hostages, and the use of "kneecappings" or "punishment shootings."

APPENDIX A

CAJ INTERVIEWS CONDUCTED IN DECEMBER 1990
(Identifying details have been removed.)

Name: X
Contact Address:

X was arrested at 6:30 on   June. Taken to Castlereagh, he saw a doctor. He was arrested in relation to the rocket attack   at which an RUC man was killed. X was told he had been named by the 4 young lads already charged for the incident. They said in their confessions that X had briefed them the night before the attack and the previous Thursday telling them where to stand and what signals to make. He was shown the 4 statements with his name marked in green ink. While he was in Castlereagh, a 5th young lad made a statement implicating him.

He was encouraged to sign a statement to make it easier for the young lads. The two detectives gave him no hassle physically but he was given threats. On the Wednesday night, the detectives interviewing him had drink taken. Apart from threats, there was little ill treatment --1st -- 2nd days.

X was told that people in West Belfast were getting away with murder. And the detectives said words to the effect that he would be walking home, drunk, from the bar one night and putting the key in the lock when somebody would get him. On the second day, they started pulling the chair away from under him. They started slapping him firmly and continuously, with hand held straight, on the back of the neck. This would go on for 10 to 15 minutes at a time. At one stage, he suddenly got 2 hard smacks full on the left side of the face.

X didn't say a word throughout all the interviews. He didn't see his solicitor for 48 hours. The detectives were becoming frustrated.

3rd Day
He didn't see a doctor again until the morning after this happened. When the first interview of the day started, the detective said, "See you're whining to the doctor," and then gave him another smack on the face. They now began hitting him on the back of the head with the base of the hand. They also began throwing a chair at him, trying to spike his legs with the legs of the chair. The threats continued. At one stage, one of the detectives asked the other, "How heavy do you think he is?" X was grabbed by the legs and the arms and lifted about 4 feet off the chair and dropped down again. "Aye, he's about nine stone." There was continuous hitting on the back of the head and poking in the ribs.

On the fourth day, the detectives started asking him to work for them. The threats got very heavy -- they weren't idle this time. "You're going for your tea this time." It was definitely the SAS or "our police unit" (undercover) that they were referring to. "Our men at the top are getting fed up with you in West Belfast. It's only a matter of our people at the top phoning somebody in the NIO and a wee man in the NIO phoning the right people. That's your death warrant." X said, "I've been threatened a million times, but this time I'm scared."

When his house was raided, the girl in the house caught a soldier planting a silver box (a decoder or something) in the yard. The detectives said they would have him for this. Remarks were also made about his file going missing during the Stevens inquiry. X told about his family getting threatening phone calls. Also, he claimed that the army had cut the phone lines on three occasions. Despite the physical ill-treatment, he made no further complaints to the doctor as there were no marks. At one stage, a detective said where he asked to see his solicitor, "Why don't you get him to do half your sentence?" They were adamant that they are going to make the five young lads cases into a show trial. His solicitor had made a complaint to the I.C.P.C.

Name: Y
Contact Address:

    Y was arrested around 5 p.m. on Wednesday   . He was arrested just after he'd got into a car outside the   Bar on Falls Road. He was arrested under s. 14 and taken to Castlereagh. When they came to the car they said "Where are you going ?" Because of this, Y refused to give his name when being signed into Castlereagh saying "Ask the one's who arrested me." A   RUC man (known locally as   ) ran in and filled in his name and address.

    He saw a doctor and told the doctor he is diabetic and needed a dose of insulin at 6 p.m. The doctor said he would have him released but the RUC refused. He didn't get insulin until his wife left his dose in at 9 p.m. Section 5 was read to him by the arresting officer and he was told he was being charged for a booby-trap car bomb, that his fingerprints had been found.

    At 9:30 p.m. to 10 p.m. he was taken for the first interview which lasted until 11:30 p.m. He was told he was going down for 20 years and asked for an explanation as to his fingerprints having been found on the bomb. Y said nothing during any of the interviews. On the Thursday morning, it was the same two detectives and nothing physical.

    In the afternoon, there were two different detectives who were verbally abusive calling him a "murdering bastard." He got continuous slaps on the head. Y stared at the video camera and had his face forced around so that he was looking at the detective.

    The evening interview was worse. Y was lifted off his chair and held by his throat against the wall. While he was sitting on the chair his legs were spun around. He was pushed back and forth on the chair. At one stage, he was pushed off the chair and stretched out his hand to support himself on the wall. He was slapped for this. He smelt alcohol off the two detectives. One detective sat on his knee and put his fingers through Y's hair. Then he opened his shirt and began pulling hairs out of his chest and arms. Later, still sitting on Y's knee, he forced Y's head down between his knees and pushed it up and down, up and down. He then went outside for two or three minutes. Came back in and sat on his knee again, putting fingers through hair and pulling Y's head down. Then he moved over and sat with his backside on Y's head and started jumping up and down. This went on for five to ten minutes. When his head was released, his neck was very sore and he couldn't hold his head up.

    At one stage, a   detective ( ) came in. He said he would show the others how to leave no marks. He held Y against the wall with the thumb and a finger of one hand on each side of his throat. "You just keep the pressure up and he'll black out." This lasted for about two minutes and Y said he felt very hot and his ears were ringing. He felt he was about to pass out. This same man slapped him on the face. This interview lasted for two and a half to three hours. There was much slapping around the face. At one stage, when a detective was

151

putting his hand through Y's hair, his hand slipped and he put a finger in Y's eye. He was continually called all the murdering bastards of the day.

He was taken back to his cell and he asked to see the doctor. He still couldn't keep his head up. The doctor said the top of his head and back of his head were very red. He gave painkillers. He also told the doctor about the alcohol. He made no complaint to the sergeant.

The same night (Thursday) he had another interview with the same two detectives. They began by commenting on him telling the doctor that they were drunk. "Well, we're drunk now" they said and began slapping his face and the back of his head. This lasted with nothing much else for two and a half to three hours. He made no complaint because he was scared.

On the Friday, the same two detectives alternated every second interview. At these interviews, he was getting prolonged quick slaps. But they didn't do much else, saying "We're not going to touch you anywhere because you're a smelly bastard." He'd had no wash and needed a shave. He was given access to his solicitor on Friday afternoon.

On the Saturday, the same sequence but not slapping. They began saying things that concerned Y. They said they were operating another internment. They would send him to jail on remand. They wanted him off the streets. They knew he would beat the charge. On another occasion, they said they would stitch him up "Not by needle and thread but by pen and paper." They claimed they were better than the English police. He was told this was because the local RUC don't like him.

He was also told that the SAS would get him one night when he was walking home from a bar. The SAS will be waiting to take you out. He was told that they knew the wee lads were innocent of the rocket attack but were determined to put them away for the older men. He was released at 10 p.m. on Saturday evening. Saw doctor before he left. He saw his doctor on the Monday - - his neck was still very sore.

Name: Z
Contact Address:

Z was lifted at 11:05 a.m. on Wednesday   just after he left his parents'
house. The house had just been raided and he had called round to see the
damage. He was given verbal and sectarian abuse on the way to Castlereagh. He
was arrested under s. 14 for the rocket attack at   which killed an RUC man.
He was taken to see a doctor.

There was no physical ill treatment on the first day. The interrogators
brought in his coat and asked him about a bag of white powder. (It was acid for
cleaning the back yard.) Z said nothing throughout all the interviews. He was
told they could substitute the powder for something else. They would stitch him
up. They made references to Guildford and Birmingham, saying he wouldn't get
the publicity. "You're just a statistic here." At the start of this first interview, Z
had moved the chair against the wall so they couldn't get behind him. He
refused to sit on the chair when they pulled it back to the center of the room.
He then sat on the floor in the corner with his back against the wall. He did this
at all subsequent interviews.

Second Interview -- the two detectives said nothing for two hours -- these
were the ones that got physical later.

Third interview -- with the first two detectives -- just threats -- he was to
be set up for loyalists. This continued for the whole first day and most of
Thursday.

Thursday evening, after tea time, the beatings started. One detective
came straight in and hit him with his elbow across the left hand side of his face
three times. Then he said to Z, "You thought you were going to get an easy
time. I'll leave no marks." He was drunk. He slapped Z across the face. He
poked Z hard in the temple with a finger 25 times. "That's how many times
you're getting shot in the head." He was screaming and bawling sectarian and
verbal abuse.

After the interview, Z asked to make a complaint. A uniformed officer
took him by the back of the neck and threw him into the cell saying "You'll have
something to complain about tomorrow." A final interview on the Thursday
night. There were matter of fact threats of death. "If we don't take you off the
streets in six months we've failed." They said they didn't care if innocent people
were with him at the time but that they would get him. All it would take was a
phone call to the NIO. They claimed this was from the very top, saying, "By
hook or by crook we'll get you." If they couldn't get him in an undercover
operation, they would set him up for loyalists.

On the Friday, Z got very disoriented. They came straight in and started
battering him, slapping his face, pulling his ears and hair. Not too badly
compared with the previous night. They weren't drunk. It was the same ones
who did all the beating. Friday night, they were drunk again. One detective,

who was   , sat on his head, then caught his head in an arm lock. The top of his head was slapped. He was head-butted and punched on the chin. The man said, "I've been doing this for 15 years. I'll not mark you." The other one was   -- he didn't touch him that night apart form five thumps to the top of his head. He said, "I'll see you tomorrow." Z got painkillers from the doctor that night and lodged a complaint.

Saturday morning, the   detective started giving him hard slaps, five alternately on each side of the face, giving out about complaints to the doctor. The other one slapped him and grabbed his throat. At one point, Z's back was sore and he lay down on the floor. They went out. When the   one came in, he ran over, screaming and bawling and grabbed Z's testicles, squeezing and lifting. The other grabbed him by the front of his shirt and the back of his neck. They both lifted him like this and began swinging him around. Z held on to the table and they dropped him on the floor so that he hurt his back. They grabbed him by his feet and lifted him trying to put his head on the chair. Z pushed the chair away and they swung him round. They pinned him against the wall by his throat, slapping and punching him in the stomach and testicles. One tried to open his mouth and spit in it but Z managed to keep his mouth closed so he didn't get the spit in. Then Z was lying on the floor again and one of them sat on top of his face and farted in his mouth. The   one was kissing him on the mouth the whole time. This interview lasted one and a half hours. The physical abuse for 45 minutes and then just threats.

At the next interview, the detectives gave no ill-treatment, just made threats about the other two.

6 p.m. Saturday, there was another interview with the detectives. They were drunk. They took Z to a bigger cell where there would be more room. He was grabbed again by the testicles very hard. They were looking for him to assault them, trying to provoke him. He was slapped on the face and had his beard pulled which was very sore. One detective said he would bring in a pair of pliers to rip the beard off his face. Z was bodily lifted by the sidelocks of his hair. One detective sat on his legs and opened his shirt. When Z tried to take his hands away, he got a big slap on the face. Big handfuls of chest hair were pulled. This was very, very painful. He was poked or jabbed in the throat forcefully. They hit his nose with the back of their hands half a dozen times. He was held with his head against the wall and given a number of short punches to the chin. There were threats "I'm an out and out loyalist from the Shankill Road. I'll pass on information." Threats also about family and friends. "You're going to bring death to them. We don't care who we kill as long as we get you."

At one stage, one of the detectives placed a chair over Z's chest as he lay on the floor. He stuck a foot into Z's testicles and started pulling his arms. This lasted for about five minutes. Z was insulted by the uniformed RUC men about making complaints. There was one more interview before he was released at 9:30 a.m. Saturday.

154

YELLOW CARD (1980)

RESTRICTED
Army Code No. 70771
Instructions for Opening Fire in Northern Ireland

General Rules
1. In all situations you are to use the minimum force necessary. FIREARMS MUST ONLY BE USED AS A LAST RESORT.
2. Your weapon must always be made safe: that is, NO live round is to be carried in the breech and in the case of automatic weapons the working parts are to be forward, unless you are ordered to carry a live round in the breech or you are about to fire.

Challenging
3. A challenge MUST be given before opening fire unless:
   a. to do so would increase the risk of death or grave injury to you or any other person.
   b. you or others in the immediate vicinity are being engaged by terrorists.
4. You are to challenge by shouting:
   'ARMY: STOP OR I FIRE' or words to that effect.

Opening Fire
5. You may only open fire against a person:
   a. if he* is committing or about to commit an act LIKELY TO ENDANGER LIFE AND THERE IS NO OTHER WAY TO PREVENT THE DANGER. The following are some examples of acts where life could be endangered, dependent always upon the circumstances:
      (1) firing or being about to fire a weapon
      (2) planting detonating or throwing an explosive device (including a petrol bomb)
      (3) deliberately driving a vehicle at a person and there is no other way of stopping him*
   b. if you know that he* has just killed or injured any person by such means and he* does not surrender if challenged and THERE IS NO OTHER WAY TO MAKE AN ARREST.

6. If you have to open fire you should:
   a. fire only aimed shots,
   b. fire no more rounds than are necessary,
   c. take all reasonable precautions not to injure anyone other than your target.

*'She' can be read instead of 'he' if applicable.

†It appears that the RUC force instructions on the use of firearms are almost identical (see *The Times*, 5 January 1983).

Source: K. Asmal (chairman), *Shoot to Kill? International Lawyers' Inquiry into the Lethal Use of Firearms by the Security Forces in Northern Ireland* (Mercier Press, 1985), pp. 75–6.

155

APPENDIX   C

DRAFT BY STANDING ADVISORY COMMISSION ON HUMAN RIGHTS OF A CODE OF
PRACTICE ON THE USE OF LETHAL FORCE BY THE SECURITY FORCES IN
NORTHERN IRELAND

GENERAL RULES

1.   In all situations the minimum force necessary must be used.
Firearms must only be used as a last resort. Where their use is
unavoidable they must be used with restraint, in proportion to the
seriousness of the offence and the legitimate objective to be
achieved, and so as to minimise damage and injury and to respect
and preserve human life.

2.   Superior officers shall ensure that members of the security
forces are equipped with appropriate self-defensive equipment and
appropriate non-lethal incapacitating weapons with a view to
restraining the use of weapons capable of causing death or serious
injury. Superior officers shall be responsible for any breach of
these rules by members of the security forces under their command
in cases in which they did not take all measures in their power to
prevent such a breach.

OPENING FIRE

3.   Firearms must always be made safe. No live rounds are to be
carried in the breach of a firearm and automatic weapons are not
to be made ready for firing unless they are about to be fired or
an express order to that effect has been given by a superior
officer.

4.   Firearms shall not be used against a person except in the
following circumstances:

   (1)   in self-defence or defence of others against the
         imminent threat of death or serious injury;

(2)   to prevent the commission of a particularly serious crime involving a grave threat to life;

(3)   to effect the arrest of a person immediately presenting such a threat.

In all these cases firearms must not be used unless there is no other way to prevent the danger and it is strictly unavoidable to protect life.

5.   The following are examples of acts endangering life, depending always on the particular circumstances:

(1)   firing or being about to fire a weapon;

(2)   planting, detonating or throwing an explosive device.

6.   In cases where the use of firearms is unavoidable the following rules must be observed:

(1)   only aimed shots are to be fired;

(2)   no more rounds than are necessary to prevent the danger referred to in rule 4 above are to be fired;

(3)   all reasonable precautions are to be taken not to injure anyone other than the person presenting that danger.

WARNING

7.   Where the use of firearms is justified in accordance with these rules members of the security forces shall identify themselves and shall give a clear warning of their intent to use firearms, with sufficient time for the warning to be observed, unless to do so would expose others or themselves to undue risk or would be clearly pointless or inappropriate in the circumstances.

8.   The words 'Army/Police: stop or I fire' or words to similar effect are to be used.

MEDICAL ATTENTION

9.   Assistance and medical aid are to be rendered to any person injured at the earliest possible moment.

INFORMING RELATIVES

10. Relatives or close friends of any person injured or affected by the use of firearms shall be notified at the earliest possible moment.

REPORTING

11. In all cases where firearms are used a report on the circumstances shall be made promptly to a superior officer.

ACCESS

12. The police shall have immediate access to a member of the security forces who has used or is reasonably suspected of having used lethal force.

Deaths caused by plastic bullets

NAME	AGE	DATE	PLACE
Stephen Geddis	10	30 August 1975	Belfast
Brian Stewart	13	10 October 1976	Belfast
Michael Donnelly	21	9 August 1980	Belfast
Paul Whitters	15	25 April 1981	Derry
Julie Livingstone	14	13 May 1981	Belfast
Carol Ann Kelly	12	22 May 1981	Belfast
Henry Duffy	45	22 May 1981	Derry
Nora McCabe	30	9 July 1981	Belfast
Peter Doherty	33	31 July 1981	Belfast
Peter McGuiness	41	9 August 1981	Belfast
Stephen McConomy	11	16 April 1982	Derry
Sean Downes	22	12 August 1984	Belfast
Keith White	20	14 April 1986	Portadown
Seamus Duffy	15	11th August 1989	Belfast

Stephen Geddis, aged 10, in Belfast. At the inquest soldiers said they fired two plastic bullets to disperse a crowd of 50-60 children who were stoning them in the Falls Road area. The boy's skull was fractured. Military witnesses did not claim he was rioting. Eyewitnesses said he was not involved in the stoning. Inquest verdict of death by misadventure.

Brian Stewart, aged 13, in Belfast. Soldiers gave evidence at the inquest of coming under heavy attack from stone-throwers in west Belfast. A corporal said he had aimed at another youth, but as he fired, he was struck by two missiles which caused him to jerk the weapon. As a result the plastic bullet hit Brian Stewart, who he said had also been throwing stones. Local people contested this, claiming there was no rioting at the time. Lord Justice Jones ruled in a civil case that the boy had been participating in a riot and that the firing of a plastic bullet was reasonable. An appeal to the European Commission of Human Rights failed.

Michael Donnelly, aged 21, August 1980, in Belfast. At the inquest soldiers said they fired 65 plastic bullets to disperse rioters in the Falls Road area. A witness said the rioting had ended before Mr Donnelly, a social worker, was hit by a plastic bullet while walking along Leeson Street. But a Royal Artillery major insisted: "No-one in my troop fired at anyone who was not throwing petrol bombs or bricks". Lord Justice Kelly said in a civil case that he accepted that the rioting was over and that there was a lull when Michael Donnelly was hit. He said the plastic bullet was fired at a time when it was "uncalled for and unjustified".

Paul Whitters, aged 15, in Derry. An independent investigation into his death conducted in 1982 by Lord Gifford, concluded that there was "no possible defence" for the boy's killing and that he had been murdered. The inquest jury found that Paul Whitters had been the ring-leader of a number of youths attempting to hijack a lorry during disturbances in Derry. Local witnesses said he could have been arrested rather than killed.

Julie Livingstone, aged 14, in Belfast. The girl was walking towards her home when hit on the head. The inquest jury described her as "an innocent victim". Plastic bullets were fired from two army Saracen troop carriers in west Belfast. A sergeant from the Royal Regiment of Wales said he had fired at a petrol bomber and had seen a youth fall.

Carol Ann Kelly, aged 12, in Belfast. The coroner found that the girl was an innocent victim who had been walking home from a shop carrying a carton of milk. The inquest found that two plastic bullets were fired from Land Rovers in an army patrol in west Belfast. Soldiers said rioting was taking place; locals said the area was quiet.

Henry Duffy, aged 45, in Derry. He was returning to his home when hit on the chest and left temple. There was no finding of rioting at the inquest which found a verdict of death by misadventure. Mr Duffy, a widower and father of seven children, was struck in the Bogside area of Derry.

Nora McCabe, aged 30, in Belfast. The jury at a second inquest found that Mrs McCabe was an innocent passer-by who had been struck on the head by a plastic bullet fired by an RUC officer. Her case led to calls from more than 70 MPs for an inquiry into the circumstances of her death. She had been on her way to buy cigarettes when she was fatally injured. Police denied that they had fired into the area in which she was shot, but the police evidence was later contradicted by a film shot by a Canadian camera crew. The inquest jury concluded that a land-rover had turned towards Linden Street, and that a plastic bullet had been fired from it.

Peter Doherty, aged 40, in Belfast. The inquest jury found that Mr Doherty was struck as he stood at the window of his third floor flat on the Falls Road. The plastic bullet was embedded in his forehead. Soldiers said petrol bombs had been thrown from the flat; this was denied by the other occupants. Two inquest juries failed to agree on what had happened.

Peter McGuinness, aged 41, in Belfast. The inquest concluded he had not been rioting, and had been telling a crowd to go away from his house when he was hit by a plastic bullet.

Stephen McConomy, aged 11, in Derry. The inquest jury concluded that the boy was one of seven or eight close to an army Saracen which was subjected to sporadic stone-throwing. A lance-corporal said he had fired at a 17 year old youth but when the smoke cleared he saw a child lying on the ground. Military witnesses did not allege the boy was a rioter and the jury, after hearing 26 witnesses, decided there was insufficient evidence that the dead boy had been involved in stone-throwing. It ruled that he had been shot at a range of 17 feet, and that the plastic bullet gun was defective, firing 11-15 inches high at a range of 10 yards.

Sean Downes, aged 22, in Belfast. The DPP decided (for the first time in a plastic bullet case) to charge the RUC officer who fired the fatal shot. He was acquitted of manslaughter in 1986. Police moved in on a sitting crowd, at a Sinn Fein rally, to arrest Martin Galvin of Noraid. Many witnesses blamed the RUC for starting the trouble. A TV film showed Sean Downes running towards police with a stick, and an officer turning to fire a plastic bullet at his chest. The judge ruled that the officer had acted "almost instinctively to defend his colleagues". The plastic bullet gun was said to be firing higher than normal. An application by Mr Downes' widow in 1988 for an inquest into his death was refused by the High Court in Belfast.

Keith White, aged 20, in Portadown. The inquest jury found Keith White was rioting. An RUC video showed him throwing stones at police following the banning of a loyalist march in Portadown. The jury said: "The deceased threw a missile and immediately turned away and was struck at the back of the head". One of the plastic bullet guns in use by police was found to be inaccurate, firing high.

Seamus Duffy, aged 15, in Belfast. The boy was killed during internment commemorations in north Belfast. His family denies he was rioting when shot. The RUC said that a police video showed the boy running away from the scene after rioting. He was reportedly shot in a street some distance away from the riot scene. His death was investigated by the RUC under the supervision of the Independent Commission for Police Complaints. The inquiry did not identify the firer of the fatal bullet, and the DPP subsequently decided against prosecution. An inquest will be held. The Duffy family has initiated a civil action against the RUC.

Source: <u>Plastic Bullets and the Law</u>. CAJ Pamphlet No. 15, 1990.   Pages 3-6.

APPENDIX E

DEATHS CAUSED BY MEMBERS OF THE SECURITY FORCES WHILE ON DUTY NOVEMBER 1982 TO SEPTEMBER 1991

Date	Description of Incident
November 11, 1982	Three men, Gervaise McKerr (31), Eugene Toman (21), and Sean Burns (21) shot dead at road check outside Lurgan; no guns found in car.
November 24, 1982	Two young men shot in a field near Oxford Island, Lurgan: Michael Tighe (17) killed and another seriously injured; three old rifles but no ammunition found at the scene.
December 12, 1982	Two men, Seamus Grew (31) and Roderick Carroll (22) shot dead after high speed chase in Armagh; no weapons found at the scene.
December 27, 1982	Patrick Elliot (19) shot dead by British Army at close range after robbery of chip shop. No paramilitary connection. No prosecution despite conflicting eye-witness statements.
January 9, 1983	Francis McColgan (31) shot dead during a car chase at Black's Road, Belfast following robbery at filling station on Lisburn Road; replica pistol found at the scene.
February 3, 1983	Two INLA members, Eugene McMonagle and Liam Duffy shot in suspicious circumstances in London/Derry. McMonagle killed. No shots fired at soldier. No weapons found at scene though soldier claimed McMonagle was armed.
March 16, 1983	William Millar (26) shot dead when police opened fire on a stolen car in the University area in Belfast; home-made sub-machine and hand-gun found in the car.

162

Date	Description of Incident
July 26, 1983	John O'Hare shot dead by RUC uniformed patrol after robbery of Lurgan Post Office/shop. Conflicting claims of stake-out. Victim was armed with sawed off shotgun.
July 30, 1983	Martin Malone, Catholic teenager, shot dead by UDR patrol in scuffle. UDR man was acquitted of manslaughter.
August 9, 1989	Thomas "Kidso" Reilly shot dead by Private Ian Thain while running from an altercation. Thain was convicted of murder and sentenced to life imprisonment. He served 2-and-a- half years.
August 13, 1983	Gerald Mallon and Brendan Convery, two INLA operatives, shot dead by RUC after carrying out armed attack on RUC constable.
November 28, 1983	During an armed raid on a Post Office in Pomeroy Co. Tyrone, Brigid Foster, a civilian pensioner, was fatally injured by an RUC bullet. Allegations of a stake-out were made.
December 4, 1983	Two IRA operatives, Colm McGirr and Brian Campbell, shot dead by SAS while approaching arms dump. Official statement claimed men were armed and refused to halt. Republican sources deny they were armed. Another man escaped.
January 30, 1984	British Army foot patrol shot dead Mark Marron in a stolen car in West Belfast. Army alleged he failed to halt. Other statements alleged the car was stationary.
February 21, 1984	The incident took place near Ballymena Co. Antrim between PIRA operatives and British undercover unit. Declan Martin and Henry Hogan were killed with allegations of coups de grace after they were injured while running away.

163

Date	Description of Incident
May 14, 1984	Seamus Fitzimmons was killed by the RUC and two colleagues in a Post Office robbery in Co. Antrim. A replica handgun was found at the scene. Allegations were made that members of the gang could have been arrested.
June 15, 1984	Paul McCann (INLA operative) and Michael Todd (RUC) shot dead in exchange of gunfire in West Belfast.
July 13, 1984	An alleged SAS ambush resulted in death of William Price and wounding of two men near Ardboe, Co. Tyrone. No official claim that the PIRA unit fired.
August 12, 1984	At an internment rally in Andersonstown, West Belfast, John Downes was killed by a plastic bullet fired at point blank range: The RUC charged a peaceful crowd when Martin Galvin began to make a speech. The RUC man who fired the bullet was subsequently cleared of unlawful killing. John Downes' widow received £25,000 compensation in October 1989.
October 19, 1984	In an undercover operation, Frederick Jackson, an uninvolved civilian, was shot by British Army personnel off the M1 near Dungannon, Co. Tyrone. The official account of Jackson's being caught in crossfire conflicted with forensic evidence that he was shot once in the back with a handgun.
December 2, 1984	Tony McBride (IRA) and Corporal Alister Slater (British Army undercover) were killed in alleged ambush near Kesh Co. Fermanagh. Another member of the IRA, Kiernan Fleming, drowned while attempting to escape.

Date	Description of Incident
December 6, 1984	In an undercover ambush in the grounds of Gransha hospital in London/Derry, William Fleming and Daniel Doherty, two IRA operatives, died after being shot. Allegations were made that no attempt was made to arrest them. Inquest jury found that the Army unit should have tried to arrest the men. 59 shots were fired.
December 17, 1984	Sean McIlvenna (IRA) was killed in a gun battle with RUC personnel after seven UDR men were wounded in a controlled explosion.
January 15, 1985	Paul Kelly was shot dead in West Belfast when the UDR opened fire on a vehicle in a joyriding incident. Witnesses alleged as many as 60 shots were fired. Four other occupants of the car were wounded.
February 7, 1985	An RUC/British Army patrol shot at a car and killed Gerard Logue in a joyriding incident in West Belfast. Inquest began without the family being informed. Contradictory statements were made by RUC and eye-witnesses.
February 23, 1985	British soldiers shot dead Charles Breslin, David Devine and Michael Devine outside Strabane. The three were members of the IRA and allegations of a shoot-to-kill policy emerged. IRA alleged an informer gave information tipping off the Army and no attempt to arrest the three was made.
February 18, 1986	Francis Bradley was shot by a British army undercover unit near Toomebridge, Co. Antrim. Bradley had no connection with paramilitaries. Reports were made that Bradley was harassed by security forces before his death. Public enquiry held by the Community for Justice concludes that Bradley's death was premeditated.
February 23, 1986	Tony Gough (IRA operative) was shot dead by a British army patrol following shooting attack on army base in Derry. Weapons recovered from the scene.

165

Date	Description of Incident
March 31, 1986	At a banned anti-Anglo-Irish Agreement parade in Portadown, Keith White was injured by an RUC plastic bullet. White died on April 14. No charges were brought.
April 26, 1986	An IRA unit was ambushed in Rosslea Co. Fermanagh while preparing an 800 lb. landmine. Seamus McElwaine was shot dead. Allegations were made that McElwaine, a Maze escaper, had been summarily executed.
September 14, 1986	A British Army patrol intercepted James McKernan who was on an IRA mission. Conflicting statements from government and IRA sources followed the shooting. Eye-witnesses said McKernan had his hands in the air when shot and could have been arrested. The inquest jury accepted the Army's version of events.
May 8, 1986	Allegations of ambush and summary execution followed the killing of eight IRA operatives as they attacked the RUC barracks at Loughgall, Co. Tyrone. The eight IRA operatives were James Lynagh, Patrick Kelly, Patrick McKearney, Declan Arthur, Sean Donnelly, Anthony Gormley, Eugene Kelly, Gerald O'Callaghan. Anthony Hughes, a civilian, was also killed in the ambush.
February 21, 1988	Aidan McAnespie was killed by a British Army bullet while crossing the border into N. Ireland at Aughnacloy, Co. Tyrone. McAnespie had been repeatedly threatened. A British soldier was fined for negligence but the manslaughter charge was dropped.

Date	Description of Incident
March 14, 1988	Kevin McCracken was shot dead by a British soldier on the evening before the funeral of the Gibraltar Three. At the inquest, it was disclosed that he had been shot in the back and was carrying an unloaded rifle. McCracken's father refused to take the witness stand in protest against the absence of the soldier who shot his son. The inquest jury commented that it was unfortunate that the soldier involved refused to attend.
July 1, 1988	An uninvolved taxi driver was killed by army bullets when an alleged SAS ambush of an IRA unit went wrong. Ken Stronge was hit while driving past N. Queen Street barracks. The soldiers opened fire, missing the IRA operatives, but hitting Stronge.
August 30, 1988	Gerard Harte, Brian Mullin, and Martin Harte were shot in an SAS-style ambush at Drumnakilly near Omagh. The three men were claimed by the IRA.
June 15, 1989	A British Marine, Adam Gilbert, was killed by a colleague in North Belfast. It was claimed that the killing was accidental and the colleague was not prosecuted.
August 9, 1989	Seamus Duffy was killed by a plastic bullet in North Belfast. The RUC claimed he was involved in rioting. A coroner's jury found he had not been rioting at the time he was shot. After an internal investigation supervised by the Independent Commission for Police Complaints, the DPP decided that no prosecutions would be brought against any RUC members.
September 9, 1989	An UVF unit were escaping after committing a sectarian murder in N. Belfast. A British army undercover unit rammed their motorcycle and shot the two men, killing Brian Robinson. Circumstances indicated that Robinson was shot dead on the ground and that the undercover unit was prepared to catch the UVF unit prior to the sectarian murder.

167

Date	Description of Incident
November 9, 1989	RUC man Ian Johnstone was killed by a fellow undercover operative in the New Lodge area of Belfast. Johnstone was a member of the RUC's SAS-trained E4A undercover squad.
January 13, 1990	John McNeill, Eddie Hale and Peter Thompson, who were robbing a bookie's establishment, were shot dead by British undercover operatives in West Belfast. John McNeill was shot while waiting in the getaway car. Replica weapons were found connected to the other two. Eye-witnesses heard no warnings and saw Hale and Thompson being shot dead on the ground after they ran out of the bookie's. The DPP directed in Dec. 1990 that there should be no prosecutions.
April 1990	Martin Corrigan, an INLA operative, was killed in Armagh during an attack on an RUC man's house. The circumstances appear consistent with an ambush by security forces.
September 30, 1990	Two teenage joy-riders, Karen Reilly and Martin Peake, were killed by a British Army patrol in West Belfast. A third teenager, Markiewicz Gorman, was injured. NIO allegations that their car had crashed a road-block were contradicted by eye-witnesses, including Markiewicz Gorman, who claimed a hail of shots were fired at the car as it was slowing down, and that there was no road-block. Six paratroopers were charged in August 1991 in connection with the incident: one with murder, three with manslaughter, and all six with conspiring to pervert the course of justice.
October 9, 1990	Desmond Grew and Martin McCaughey were shot dead in an undercover-style ambush by British operatives. The men were claimed by the IRA. Three people reportedly arrested at the scene and charged with possession of weapons subsequently had all charges against them dropped in June 1991.

Date	Description of Incident
November 12, 1990	Alexander Patterson, an INLA operative, was shot dead by British undercover soldiers near Strabane Co. Tyrone. Official reports claimed an exchange of gunfire took place. Others were arrested after what appeared to be an attack on the home of a UDR man was foiled. A Panorama programme screened in July claimed that Patterson was an RUC informer and was shot as he sat in his car waiting for the security forces to arrive after the shooting had stopped.
December 30, 1990	British marines opened fire on a car in disputed circumstances in Cullyhanna, Co. Armagh. The army claimed that the car broke through a checkpoint. Eyewitnesses claimed the soldiers opened fire without provocation. Fergal Caraher was killed and his brother Michael was seriously injured.
April 10, 1991	Colm Marks was shot three times by the RUC in Downpatrick. A rocket launcher was found "close to the scene." Subsequent reports disputed whether he was a threat to the police officers at the moment he was shot. Other allegations involved a delay in bringing him to the hospital.
June 3, 1991	Lawrence McNally, Michael Ryan and Tony Doris were killed by British undercover operatives in the main street of Coagh, Co. Tyrone. The attack happened at 7:30 a.m. The bodies were, according to press reports, burned beyond recognition after the car crashed, exploding into flames, following some ten minutes of gunfire.

Source: Committee on the Administration of Justice, 1991.

Security Force Prosecutions

Case	Victim	Verdict
Army		
R. v. Foxford[a] (1974)	Kevin Heatley	Not Guilty
R. v. Ross (1974)	Anthony Mitchell	Not Guilty
R. v. Spencer (1974)	Samuel Martin	Not Guilty
R. v. Nicholl (1975)	Alex Howell	Not Guilty
R. v. Jones (1975)	Patrick McElhone	Not Guilty
R. v. Fury (1975)	Hugh Devine	Not Guilty
R. v. Scott (1976)	Anthony Gallagher	Not Guilty
R. v. Williams (1977)	Majella O'Hare	Not Guilty
R. v. Bohan and Temperley (1979)	John Boyle	Not Guilty
R. v. Davidson[b] (1981)	Theresa Donaghey	Guilty (Manslaughter)
R. v. Bailey and Jones (1983)	Eamonn Bradley	Not Guilty
R. v. Thain (1984)	Thomas Reilly	Guilty (Murder)
RUC		
R. v. McKeown (1981)	Michael McCartan	Not Guilty
R. v. Robinson (1984)	Seamus Grew, Roddy Carroll	Not Guilty
R. v. Montgomery, Brannigan and Robinson (1984)	Gervais McKerr, Eugene Toman, Sean Burns	Not Guilty
R. v. Hegarty (1987)	John Downes	Not Guilty
UDR		
R. v. Baird (1984)	Martin Malone	Not Guilty

The acquittal rate in no-jury courts in 1981 was 33.98 per cent and 34.92 per cent in 1982 (The Baker Report, Appendix H, page 160). The acquittal rate in prosecutions of members of the security forces for killings committed whilst on duty resulting from the use of firearms is 90.5 per cent overall.

This table does not include prosecutions for offences committed whilst off duty or caused other than by the use of firearms (K. Asmal, *Shoot to Kill?*, p. 25, n. 25). Thus the convictions of four UDR men in 1986 for murdering Adrian Carroll are not included.

(a) This defendant was convicted of manslaughter by Kelly J. at first instance but his conviction was overturned on appeal by Lord Lowry C.J.

(b) Sentenced to 12 months' detention in Young Offenders' Centre, suspended for 2 years.

Source: Justice Under Fire, Anthony Jennings, editor. Pluto Press, London, 1990. Page 105.

PRINCIPLES ON THE EFFECTIVE PREVENTION AND INVESTIGATION OF EXTRA-LEGAL, ARBITRARY AND SUMMARY EXECUTIONS

Adopted by the Economic and Social Council by its resolution 1989/65 of 24 May 1989, on the recommendation of the Committee on Crime Prevention and Control at its tenth session (Vienna 1988).

Prevention

1.   Governments shall prohibit by law all extra-legal, arbitrary and summary executions and shall ensure that any such executions are recognized as offenses under their criminal laws, and are punishable by appropriate penalties which take into account the seriousness of such offenses. Exceptional circumstances, including a state of war or threat of war, internal political instability or any other public emergency, may not be invoked as a justification of such executions. Such executions shall not be carried out under any circumstances including, but not limited to, situations of internal armed conflict, excessive or illegal use of force by a public official or other person acting in an official capacity, or a person acting at the instigation, or with the consent or acquiescence of such person, and situations in which deaths occur in custody. This prohibition shall prevail over decrees issued by governmental authority.

2.   In order to prevent extra-legal, arbitrary and summary executions, Governments shall ensure strict control, including a clear chain of command over all officials responsible for the apprehension, arrest, detention, custody and imprisonment as well as those officials authorized by law to use force and firearms.

3.   Governments shall prohibit orders from superior officers or public authorities authorizing or inciting other persons to carry out any such extra-legal, arbitrary or summary executions. All persons shall have the right and the duty to defy such orders. Training of law enforcement officials shall emphasize the above provisions.

4.   Effective protection through judicial or other means shall be guaranteed to individuals and groups who are in danger of extra-legal, arbitrary or summary executions, including those who receive death threats.

5.   No one shall be involuntarily returned or extradited to a country where there are substantial grounds for believing that he or she may become a victim of extra-legal, arbitrary or summary execution in that country.

6.   Governments shall ensure that persons deprived of their liberty are held in officially recognized places of custody, and that accurate information on their custody and whereabouts, including transfers, is made promptly available to their relatives and lawyer or other persons of confidence.

7.   Qualified inspectors, including medical personnel, or an equivalent independent authority, shall conduct inspections in places of custody on a regular basis, and be empowered to undertake unannounced inspections on their own initiative, with full guarantees of independence in the exercise of this function. The inspectors shall have unrestricted access to all persons in such places of custody, as well as to all their records.

8.   Governments shall make every effort to prevent extra-legal, arbitrary and summary executions through measures such as diplomatic intercession, improved access of complainants to intergovernmental and judicial bodies, and public denunciation. Intergovernmental mechanisms

shall be used to investigate reports of any such executions, and to take effective action against such practices. Governments, including those of countries where extra-legal, arbitrary and summary executions are reasonably suspected to occur, shall co-operate fully in international investigations on the subject.

Investigation

9. There shall be a thorough, prompt and impartial investigation of all suspected cases of extra-legal, arbitrary and summary executions, including cases where complaints by relatives or other reliable reports suggest unnatural death in the above circumstances. Governments shall maintain investigative offices and procedures to undertake such inquiries. The purpose of the investigation shall be to determine the cause, manner and time of death, the person responsible, and any adequate autopsy, the collection and analysis of all physical and documentary evidence, and statements from witnesses. The investigation shall distinguish between natural death, accidental death, suicide and homicide.

10. The investigative authority shall have the power to obtain all the information necessary to the inquiry. Those persons conducting the investigation shall have at their disposal all the necessary budgetary and technical resources for effective investigation. They shall also have the authority to oblige officials allegedly involved in any such executions to appear and testify. The same shall apply to any witness. To this end, they shall be entitled to issue summons to witnesses including the officials allegedly involved, and to demand the production of evidence.

11. In cases in which the established investigative procedures are inadequate because of lack of expertise or impartiality, because of the importance of the matter or because of the apparent existence of a pattern of abuse, and in cases where there are complaints from the family of the victim about these inadequacies or other substantial reasons, Governments shall pursue investigations through an independent commission of inquiry or similar procedure. Members of such a commission shall be chosen for their recognized impartiality, competence and independence as individuals. In particular, they shall be independent of any institution, agency or person that may be the subject of the inquiry. The commission shall have the authority to obtain all information necessary to the inquiry and shall conduct the inquiry as provided under these Principles.

12. The body of the deceased person shall not be disposed of until an adequate autopsy is conducted by a physician, who shall, if possible, be an expert in forensic pathology. Those conducting the autopsy shall have the right of access to all investigative data, to the place where the body was discovered, and to the place where the death is thought to have occurred. If the body has been buried and it later appears that an investigation is required, the body shall be promptly and competently exhumed for an autopsy. If skeletal remains are discovered, they should be carefully exhumed and studied according to systematic anthropological techniques.

13. The body of the deceased shall be available to those conducting the autopsy for a sufficient amount of time to enable a thorough investigation to be carried out. The autopsy shall, at a minimum, attempt to establish the identity of the deceased and the cause and manner of death. The time and place of death shall also be determined to the extent possible. Detailed color photographs of the deceased shall be included in the autopsy report in order to document and support the findings of the investigation. The autopsy report must describe any and all injuries to the deceased, including any evidence of torture.

14. In order to ensure objective results, those conducting the autopsy must be able to function impartially and independently of any potentially implicated persons or organizations or entities.

15. Complainants, witnesses, those conducting the investigation and their families shall be protected from violence, threats of violence or any other form of intimidation. Those potentially implicated in extra-legal, arbitrary or summary executions shall be removed from any position of control or power, whether direct or indirect, over complainants, witnesses and their families, as well as over those conducting investigations.

16. Families of the deceased and their legal representatives shall be informed of, and have access to, any hearing as well as to all information relevant to the investigation, and shall be entitled to present other evidence. The family of the deceased shall have the right to insist that a medical or other qualified representative be present at the autopsy. When the identity of a deceased person has been determined, a notification of death shall be posted, and the family or relatives of the deceased immediately informed. The body of the deceased shall be returned to them upon completion of the investigation.

17. A written report shall be made within a reasonable period of time on the methods and findings of such investigations. The report shall be made public immediately and shall include the scope of the inquiry, procedures and methods used to evaluate evidence as well as conclusions and recommendations based on findings of fact and on applicable law. The report shall also describe in detail specific events that were found to have occurred, and the evidence upon which such findings were based, and list the names of witnesses who testified, with the exception of those whose identities have been withheld for their own protection. The Government shall, within a reasonable period of time, either reply to the report of the investigation, or indicate the steps to be taken in response to it.

Legal Proceedings

18. Governments shall ensure that persons identified by the investigation as having participated in extra-legal, arbitrary and summary executions in any territory under their jurisdiction are brought to justice. Governments shall either bring such persons to justice or co-operate to extradite any such persons to other countries wishing to exercise jurisdiction. This principle shall apply irrespective of who and where the perpetrators or the victims are, their nationalities or where the offence was committed.

19. Without prejudice to Principle 3 above, an order from a superior officer or a public authority may not be invoked as a justification for extra-legal, arbitrary or summary executions. Superiors, officers or other public officials may be held responsible for acts committed by officials under their hierarchical authority if they had a reasonable opportunity to prevent such acts. In no circumstances, including a state of war, siege or other public emergency, shall blanket immunity from prosecution be granted to any person allegedly involved in extra-legal, arbitrary or summary executions.

20. The families and dependents of victims of extra-legal, arbitrary and summary executions shall be entitled to fair and adequate compensation, within a reasonable period of time.

NORTHERN IRELAND (EMERGENCY PROVISIONS) ACT 1978

THE SCHEDULED OFFENCES

PART I

SUBSTANTIVE OFFENCES

Common law offences

1. Murder, subject to note 1 below.

2. Manslaughter, subject to note 1 below.

3. The common law offence of riot.

4. Kidnapping[, subject to note 1 below].

5. False imprisonment[, subject to note 1 below].

6. Assault occasioning actual bodily harm, subject to note 1 below.

Malicious Damage Act 1861

7. Offences under section 35 of the Malicious Damage Act 1861 (interference with railway)[, subject to note 2 below].

Offences against the Person Act 1861

8. Offences under the following provisions of the Offences against the Person Act 1861, subject as mentioned below,—

    (*a*) section 4 (conspiracy, etc. to murder) subject to note 2 below;

    (*b*) section 16 (threats to kill) subject to note 2 below;

    (*c*) section 18 (wounding with intent to cause grievous bodily harm) subject to note 2 below;

    (*d*) section 20 (causing grievous bodily harm) subject to note 2 below;

    (*e*) section 28 (causing grievous bodily harm by explosives);

    (*f*) section 29 (causing explosion or sending explosive substance or throwing corrosive liquid with intent to cause grievous bodily harm);

    (*g*) section 30 (placing explosive near building or ship with intent to do bodily injury).

Explosive Substances Act 1883

9. Offences under the following provisions of the Explosive Substances Act 1883—

  (*a*) section 2 (causing explosion likely to endanger life or damage property);
  (*b*) section 3 (attempting to cause any such explosion, and making or possessing explosive with intent to endanger life or cause serious damage to property);
  (*c*) section 4 (making or possessing explosives in suspicious circumstances).

Prison Act (Northern Ireland) 1953

10. Offences under the following provisions of the Prison Act (Northern Ireland) 1953, subject to note 2 below,—

  (*a*) section 25 (being unlawfully at large while under sentence);
  (*b*) section 26 (escaping from lawful custody and failing to surrender to bail);
  (*c*) section 27 (attempting to break prison);
  (*d*) section 28 (breaking prison by force or violence);
  (*e*) section 29 (rescuing or assisting or permitting to escape from lawful custody persons under sentence of death or life imprisonment);
  (*f*) section 30 (rescuing or assisting or permitting to escape from lawful custody persons other than persons under sentence of death or life imprisonment);
  (*g*) section 32 (causing discharge of prisoner under pretended authority);
  (*h*) section 33 (assisting prisoners to escape by conveying things into prisons).

Firearms Act (Northern Ireland) 1969

11. ...

Theft Act (Northern Ireland) 1969

12. Offences under the following provisions of the Theft Act (Northern Ireland) 1969, subject to *note 4* below,—

  (*a*) section 8 (robbery);
  (*b*) section 10 (aggravated burglary).

Protection of the Person and Property Act (Northern Ireland) 1969

13. Offences under the following provisions of the Protection of the Person and Property Act (Northern Ireland) 1969—

  (*a*) section 1 (intimidation)[, subject to note 2 below];
  (*b*) section 2 (making or possessing petrol bomb, etc. in suspicious circumstances);
  (*c*) section 3 (throwing or using petrol bomb, etc.).

Hijacking

14. Offences under section 1 of [the Aviation Security Act 1982] (aircraft).

15. Offences in Northern Ireland under section 2 of the Criminal Jurisdiction Act 1975 (vehicles and ships).

[Prevention of Terrorism (Temporary Provisions) Act 1984]

16. Offences under the following provisions of the [Prevention of Terrorism (Temporary Provisions) Act 1984]—

  (*a*) section 9 (breach of exclusion orders);
  (*b*) section 10 (contributions towards acts of terrorism);
  (*c*) section 11 (information about acts of terrorism).

Criminal Damage (Northern Ireland) Order 1977

17. Offences under the following provisions of the Criminal Damage (Northern Ireland) Order 1977, subject to note 2 below—

  (*a*) Article 3(1) and (3) or Article 3(2) and (3) (arson);
  (*b*) Article 3(2) (destroying or damaging property with intent to endanger life);
  (*c*) Article 4 (threats to destroy or damage property);
  (*d*) Article 5 (possessing anything with intent to destroy or damage property).

18. Offences under Article 3 of the Criminal Law (Amendment) (Northern Ireland) Order 1977 (bomb hoaxes), subject to note 2 below.

This Act

19. Offences under the following provisions of this Act—

   (a) section 21;
   (b) section 22;
   (c) section 23;
   (d) paragraph 13 of Schedule 1.

[The Firearms (Northern Ireland) Order 1981

19A. Offences under the following provisions of the Firearms (Northern Ireland) Order 1981—

   (a) Article 3(1) (possessing, purchasing or acquiring firearm or ammunition without certificate)[,subject to note 2 below];
   (b) Article 4(1), (2), (3) or (4) (manufacturing, dealing in, repairing, etc, firearm or ammunition without being registered)[, subject to note 2 below];
   (c) Article 5 (shortening barrel of shot gun or converting imitation firearm into firearm)[, subject to note 2 below];
   (d) Article 6(1) (manufacturing, dealing in or possessing machine gun, or weapon discharging, or ammunition containing, noxious substance)[, subject to note 2 below];
   (e) Article 17 (possessing firearm or ammunition with intent to endanger life or cause serious damage to property);
   (f) Article 18 (use or attempted use of firearm or imitation firearm to prevent arrest of self or another, etc);
   (g) Article 19 (carrying firearm or imitation firearm with intent to commit indictable offence or prevent arrest of self or another);
   (h) Article 20(1) (carrying firearm, etc, in public place)[, subject to notes 2 and 3 below];
   (i) Article 22 (possession of firearm or ammunition by person who has been sentenced to imprisonment, etc, and sale of firearm or ammunition to such a person)[, subject to note 2 below];
   (j) Article 23 (possessing firearm or ammunition in suspicious circumstances).]

[Taking of Hostages Act 1982

19A. Offences under the Taking of Hostages Act 1982.]

NOTES

1. Murder, manslaughter[, kidnapping, false imprisonment] or an assault occasioning actual bodily harm is not a scheduled offence in any particular case in which the Attorney General for Northern Ireland certifies that it is not to be treated as a scheduled offence.

[2. An offence under—

   (a) section 35 of the Malicious Damage Act 1861; or
   (b) section 4, 16, 18 or 20 of the Offences Against the Person Act 1861; or
   (c) section 25, 26, 27, 28, 29, 30, 32 or 33 of the Prison Act (Northern Ireland) 1953; or
   (d) section 1 of the Protection of the Person and Property Act (Northern Ireland) 1969; or
   (e) Article 3, 4 or 5 of the Criminal Damage (Northern Ireland) Order 1977; or
   (f) Article 3 of the Criminal Law (Amendment) (Northern Ireland) Order 1977; or
   (g) Article 3, 4, 5, 6, 20 or 22 of the Firearms (Northern Ireland) Order 1981,

is not a scheduled offence in any particular case in which the Attorney General for Northern Ireland certifies that it is not be treated as a scheduled offence.]

3. An offence under [article 20(1) of the Firearms (Northern Ireland) Order 1981] is a scheduled offence only where it is charged that the offence relates to a weapon other than an air weapon.

4. Robbery and aggravated burglary are scheduled offences only where it is charged that an explosive, firearm, imitation firearm or weapon of offence was used to commit the offence; and expressions defined in section 10 of the Theft Act (Northern Ireland) 1969 have the same meaning when used in this note.

PART II
INCHOATE AND RELATED OFFENCES

20. Each of the following offences, that is to say—

> (a) aiding, abetting, counselling, procuring or inciting the commission of an offence specified in Part I of this Schedule (hereafter in this paragraph referred to as a "substantive offence");
>
> (b) attempting or conspiring to commit a substantive offence;
>
> (c) an offence under section 4 of the Criminal Law Act (Northern Ireland) 1967 of doing any act with intent to impede the arrest or prosecution of a person who has committed a substantive offence;
>
> (d) an offence under section 5(1) of the Criminal Law Act (Northern Ireland) 1967 of failing to give information to a constable which is likely to secure, or to be of material assistance in securing the apprehension, prosecution or conviction of a person for a substantive offence,

shall be treated for the purposes of this Act as if it were the substantive offence.

PART III
EXTRA-TERRITORIAL OFFENCES

21. Any extra-territorial offence as defined in section 1 of the Criminal Jurisdiction Act 1975.

NOTES

The words in square brackets at the end of paras 4, 5, 7, 13(a), 19A(a), (b), (c), (d), (i) were added, the words in square brackets in para 19A(h), and note 2, were substituted, and the words in square brackets in note 1 were inserted, by the Northern Ireland (Emergency Provisions) Act 1978 (Amendment) Order 1986, SI 1986/75.

Para 11 was repealed, the first para 19A was inserted, and the words in square brackets in note 3 were substituted, by the Firearms (Northern Ireland) Order 1981, SI 1981/155, art 61, Sch 4, para 4(a), Sch 5.

The words in square brackets in para 14 were substituted by the Aviation Security Act 1982, s 40, Sch 2, para 6.

The words in square brackets in para 16 and the heading to that paragraph were substituted by the Prevention of Terrorism (Temporary Provisions) Act 1984, s 14, Sch 3, Pt III, para 8.

The second para 19A was inserted by the Taking of Hostages Act 1982, s 2(3); see further as to that paragraph, the note "Prospective amendments" below.

Prospective amendments. The following amendments are made to this Schedule by the Nuclear Material (Offences) Act 1983, s 4(3), as from a day to be appointed under s 8(2) thereof, Vol 12, title Criminal Law:

> (i) in para 12, the words "notes 4 and 5" are substituted for the words "note 4", and the following paragraphs are added:
>
> "(c) section 1 (theft);
> (d) section 9 (burglary);
> (e) section 15 (obtaining property by deception);
> (f) section 20 (blackmail)."

> (ii) The second para 19A is re-numbered 19B and the following para 19C is inserted:

"Nuclear Material (Offences) Act 1983

19C. Offences under section 2 of the Nuclear Material (Offences) Act 1983 (offences involving nuclear material: preparatory acts and threats)".

> (iii) The following notes 4 and 5 are substituted for note 4 above:

"4. Robbery and aggravated burglary are scheduled offences only where it is charged—

> (a) that an explosive, firearm, imitation firearm or weapon of offence was used to commit the offence; or
>
> (b) that the offence was committed in relation to or by means of nuclear material within the meaning of the Nuclear Material (Offences) Act 1983;

and expressions defined in section 10 of the Theft Act (Northern Ireland) 1969 have the same meaning when used in this note.

5. An offence under section 1, 9, 15 or 20 of the Theft Act (Northern Ireland) 1969 is a scheduled offence only where it is charged that the offence was committed in relation to or by means of nuclear material within the meaning of the Nuclear Material (Offences) Act 1983."

Attorney General for Northern Ireland. That office is now held by the Attorney General for England and Wales; see the Northern Ireland Constitution Act 1973, s 10, this part of this title ante.

Duration. As to the duration of Pts I, II of this Schedule, see s 33(2), (3) ante and the orders noted thereto.

Malicious Damage Act 1861, s 35; Offences against the Person Act 1861, ss 4, 16, 18, 20, 28–30; Explosive Substances Act 1883, ss 2–4. See Vol 12, title Criminal Law; as to amendments applying to Northern Ireland, see the Introductory Notes to those Acts.

Prison Act (Northern Ireland) 1953. 1953 c 18 (NI); not printed in this work.

Firearms Act (Northern Ireland) 1969. 1969 c 12 (NI); repealed and replaced by the Firearms (Northern Ireland) Order 1981, SI 1981/155.

Theft Act (Northern Ireland) 1969. 1969 c 16 (NI); not printed in this work.

Protection of the Person and Property Act (Northern Ireland) 1969. 1969 c 29 (NI); not printed in this work.

Aviation Security Act 1982, s 1. See Vol 4, title Aviation.

Criminal Jurisdiction Act 1975, ss 1, 2. See this part of this title ante.

Prevention of Terrorism (Temporary Provisions) Act 1984. See Vol 12, title Criminal Law.

Criminal Damage (Northern Ireland) Order 1977. SI 1977/426 (made under the Northern Ireland Act 1974, Sch 1, para 1, this part of this title ante), as amended.

Criminal Law (Amendment) (Northern Ireland) Order 1977. SI 1977/1249 (made under the Northern Ireland Act 1974, Sch 1, para 1, this part of this title ante), as amended.

Firearms (Northern Ireland) Order 1981. SI 1981/155 (made under the Northern Ireland Act 1974, Sch 1, para 1, this part of this title ante), as amended.

Taking of Hostages Act 1982. See Vol 12, title Criminal Law.

Criminal Law Act (Northern Ireland) Act 1967. 1967 c 18 (NI); not printed in this work.

APPENDIX I

Threats, Verbal Abuse and Derogatory Remarks Made by R.U.C. About Solicitors at Police Stations 1989-1991

1989

Client	Police Station	Date	From Statement
A	Castlereagh	5/1	"They also said that I was probably involved in the Falls Bath explosion and wondered if Finucane would defend me so strenuously for that since two nationalists were killed."
B	Castlereagh	5/1	"He asked me if I had seen Finucane purposely pronouncing the name incorrectly and spitting having said it. He then responded by saying, 'I bet you fucking haven't because there isn't enough money in it for him to come here. The only thing that bastard is concerned with is money and if he doesn't bother his arse the first thing he will do is ask you to sign two or three documents so he gets the money while you go to jail.' He explained that Mr. Finucane at the start will plead 'Not Guilty' and then change the plea to 'Guilty.' He asked me if I knew why. He said, 'Everything knows why, even the judge' and went on to explain that if Mr. Finucane pleads 'Not Guilty' he receives £5,000 - £6,000 where as on the other hand he pleads 'Guilty' he receives £1,500. Therefore, he will do the same to you having got his £6,000. They also informed me to change my solicitor for it was quite evident they didn't care if he still hadn't come to visit me. He also began to hurl abuse at his partner telling how he was every bit as bad if not worse. They insisted my solicitor was a waster, the proof being that he couldn't get his brother off therefore how is he going to get me off. He informed me that my solicitor was working for the I.R.A., he would meet

his end also. He informed me that I wasn't high enough in the I.R.A. and that's the reason why I wasn't coming rushing. This interview was interrupted by a uniformed policeman who brought me to see my solicitor who I informed of the abuse. I informed him that I was afraid to make any further complaints and he told me he would have to. He asked me who did I think I was, sitting down, and said I have obviously been talking to that dickhead Pat Finucane. He said, 'Is that the best he can do for you? I'll tell you to sit down.' He went on to say that it was obvious that he hadn't even the power to do that. He asked me would I give Mr. Finucane a message from him. The message was that you judge a person's character by his company and Mr. Finucane's company was made up of murderers, blackmailers, gangsters, etc. He told me to tell him that he is a thug in a suit, a person trying to let on he is doing a job and that he, like every other fenian bastard, would meet his end. He told me that he could have a good solicitor in a number of hours. He yelled and screamed shouting that this racket would only come to a halt if I signed the statement admitting my guilt and if I wasn't guilty Finucane wouldn't get his £6,000 and I would get off. He told me he believed Finucane would brainwash me to sue for wrongful arrest so as he could get more money but insisted that it would never work for there wasn't a mark on me. This was to tell me that Finucane hadn't done me much good and that I was on my way to Crumlin Road. Another unusual thing happened, after my visit with my solicitor Mr. Patrick Finucane, I was searched. There was a more thorough search than on my arrival. Inspector said, 'We don't necessarily have to put you to jail. We have ways and means of dealing with yourself and your friendly Mr.

Pat.' They also mentioned about lining for a coffin. The fat man also mentioned my solicitor. I think it was the third after Pat Finucane's visit. He said that me and Pat Finucane and my father would have at the most five years to live. He said that it might be as little as two years but might be five years but not to worry if they are still living after two years we would still get them. The first interview after Pat's visit, the fat man told me to sit down. I sat down and the fat fellow said that Pat Finucane had mentioned about rights and I was to forget about it. Pat Finucane had told me that when I went into the interview room just to sit down and if they told me to stand just to remain sitting. The fat fella told me not to worry about what Pat Finucane said."

C	Castlereagh	25/1	"They made derogatory remarks about my solicitor Mr. Finucane."
D	Castlereagh	29/1	"They said the solicitor was an I.R.A. man in a suit, another provie on their payroll, the solicitor didn't give a damn about me and he was looking after the ones who put the stuff there. They said the solicitor was just telling me to sit there and say nothing. He deals with all the hoods. They are betting on who my solicitor would be and said Patrick Finucane and said that my father would be involved in getting Patrick Finucane. They told me that no solicitor had phoned in and that I had simply no rights. They advised me not to get an I.R.A. solicitor and they gave me a list of solicitors that would do me far better. They said that they were hoping that Mr. Finucane instructed me to say nothing because they had an ace up their sleeves. He again said that having an I.R.A. solicitor would beat me. He said that Mr. Finucane only represented provisionals and that I was not high enough up in it to be trusted."

181

E	Castlereagh	20/3	"References made about Pat again along the lines that he made a good living out of the troubles and got himself a high profile."
F	Castlereagh	21/3	"At the third interview they shouted in, 'the solicitor's visit, Finucane's here.' One said it was a bit of a loss, referring to Pat Finucane's killing."
G	Castlereagh	7/4	"Asked for solicitor from Madden & Finucane. I think I said Kevin Winters. C.I.D. said, 'Finucane is dead, anyone you get in contact with is dead as well.'"
H	Castlereagh	8/8	"They said it was no good seeing a solicitor. I would have to give it now referring to statement. They said that when I see my solicitor, my solicitor will advise me to say nothing and that would do me no good."
I	Castlereagh	11/89	"During my first interview, when I asked for Madden & Finucane, they said that I hardly wanted Finucane because he was finished and they said that Cullen had seen the same solicitor and I presume he knew about it anyway. They said that Pat Finucane was a bastard and that it was a good job well done and he deserved it. He said that no one had been charged and no one would be charged. He said that Mr. Madden and those with him would have to watch out. They said that Oliver Kelly and Paddy McGrory however would be the next two to get it and it was their turn to come shortly. Detective Black said on Friday, last interview before lunch between 11:00 a.m. and 12:45 p.m., that my consultation which was supervised with my solicitor had been taped and that they had a transcript of it and that McMenamin would end up in Castlereagh on a charge of collecting details of security forces likely to be useful to terrorists, he seemed quite angry about this."

Client	Police Station	Date	From Statement

J   Castlereagh   20/12   "They said that my solicitor would get in and say that I was doing a good job and pat me on the back and that he would tell me to say nothing. After I saw my solicitor, the interviewing detective made smart remarks and said something like, 'I suppose he gave you a pat on the back and told you to remain silent' and that I was doing well. One of them said Pat was a real gentleman and that he knew him personally."

1990

Client	Police Station	Date	From Statement
A	Castlereagh	7/1	"When I was being processed at Castlereagh Holding Center on Sunday evening, the policeman at reception asked me did I want a solicitor. I indicated that I wanted Madden & Finucane and one of the ordinary policemen who had escorted me passed a comment saying something like, 'It will have to be fucking Madden, it'll hardly be that other cunt.'"
B	Castlereagh	15/1	"They mentioned Mr. Finucane and said that Loyalists killed him and they said that Madden & Finucane would advise him not to talk to the police...they said that once my solicitor came up to see them all I would be doing would be signing legal forms. They said that that was all the solicitor was interested in -- signing legal aid forms and getting away as soon as possible. They said that if I applied for legal aid, the legal aid would be revoked and that they couldn't even make a bail application. One of them said that the solicitors just hoped that I would be kept in for seven days because it would be worth more money... They referred to my solicitor Peter Madden and referred to

183

him as 'A dirty provo scumbag and that he should be getting the same as Pat.' I should say that in one of the interviews after I saw my solicitor, the C.I.D. noted that I wasn't seen by Peter Madden but by Kevin Winters and he said something like, 'It wasn't Madden, it was Kevin Winters, ah sure he's only a fucking wanker anyway.'"

C	Grosvenor Rd.	16/1	"They mentioned briefly about my solicitor. One of the policemen said that it used to be Madden & Finucane, now it's just Madden."
D	Antrim Rd.	25/1	"They asked me yesterday why I had Madden & Finucane as my solicitors. They said to me that my solicitor would go and tell the R.A. about it. They said that these solicitors were no good to me. They advised me to use another solicitor. They said that they would speak to the I.R.A."
E	Castlereagh	7/1	"They told me that when I saw my solicitor there would be a supervised visit with an inspector present. They said that the reason for this was because they didn't want any illegal conversations taking place... They asked me did I see my solicitor. They said that it didn't matter anyway because it was all taped. The persons who said this were Lynas and Balhan or Baldwin, I'm not sure of the exact spelling."
F	Castlereagh	21/2	"They said that Finucane was on the phone and that I must be in the I.R.A. They said that they work for the I.R.A. After they said this, I told them that I didn't want to see a solicitor then."
G	Castlereagh	23/2	"The only time I spoke was to tell them that I wanted to see my solicitor Kevin Winters. They asked me did I know Kevin Winters. I didn't answer them. They said that all the solicitors were interested in were the legal

aid forms."

H	Woodbourne	12/2	"They said that my solicitor was only in it for the money. They went on about my solicitor advising me to remain silent but that it wouldn't get me anywhere."
I	Castlereagh	5/2	"They asked me the name of the solicitor during the interview and said Mr. Madden & Co. They laughed at this."
J	Castlereagh	22/3	"They told me not to listen to my solicitor. They said that I shouldn't listen to him because he wouldn't be doing time. They said that I must have been afraid of the provies."
K	Castlereagh	7/3	"They said that's not a smart move getting the R.A.'s solicitor Madden & Finucane. They said he doesn't give a fuck about you, he's just up here to get his £30-£40."
L	Castlereagh	5/3	"They mentioned to me that Mr. Winters or Mr. Madden would say that we the police must have planted forensics on the coat and then when it came to trial this was what we would say happened."
M	Castlereagh	29/4	"Whenever I told them who my solicitors were they said things like 'Oh, others must have told you to use Madden & Finucane.'"
N	Castlereagh	27/4	"They said come today in the afternoon that I was stupid doing that. They were referring to a Habeas Corpus application which my solicitor brought and they are saying that it is a silly thing to do. They said that if I went ahead with it I could do a month in prison. After I had seen my solicitor this morning, I noticed that during the subsequent interviews the police were extra careful in the notes they were writing out...they also mentioned Pat Finucane and said that my

solicitor was a wanker...they were also very abusive about the fact that my solicitor advised me to take a Habeas Corpus application."

O	Castlereagh	13/4	"The solicitor had better be God because that is the only way you are getting out of this caper. ...said I should change my solicitor, he is not going to do your time for you."
P	Castlereagh	9/4	"After the legal visit yesterday, one of the detectives said, 'That's Madden, he was only here twenty minutes, he usually stays an hour. I bet you he is shitting himself after Finucane got it. He's probably got security around his house."
Q	Castlereagh	3/4	"They mentioned the late Mr. Finucane."
R	Castlereagh	3/4	"They said something like, 'They didn't know who my solicitor was, but whoever it was he was talking a load of shit and advising me to remain silent...' They went on again about my solicitor advising me wrongly. They said that because of this I was going to go to jail. They said that my solicitor was only in it for the money and that he was not concerned .... They mentioned about the fact that my solicitor didn't call on Friday 6th April 1990, they said that he didn't give a fuck. They said that I must not have told my solicitor everything because he would have advised me to talk to them. They said that if I had told him everything, then he would have been giving different advice."
S	Castlereagh	3/4	"Today they have been talking about the inner circle. They mentioned the late Mr. Finucane. They said that they may as well get the road sweeps moving to get the scum off and the dirt off out of the road."

T	Castlereagh	23/5	"They made various comments that solicitors only come up any way for the legal aid and then go. They also asked me why I asked for Madden & Finucane, saying that suppose you were told to ask for them."
U	Castlereagh	8/5	"This fresh C.I.D. man was aggressive and threatening. He stated that I deserved to be dead. He referred to Pat as 'Pat the rat.' He said that I was lower than a snake and that I only operated in the darkness of the night. He said that if he had his way, I would be dead just the way Pat got it...He asked me how Pat looked after being shot but stated that he was probably all patched up by the time I saw him. He threatened to get gory photographs of his body after having been shot... They said that I.R.A. violence was responsible for Pat's death. I think that one of them was a free mason of passing references made to Pat's partner and their role in assisting the I.R.A."
V	Castlereagh	2/5	"They made some brief derogatory remarks abut Pat Finucane. They said something about him...before being transferred to Strandtown this morning a Chief Superintendent asked me did I want anyone contacted. I said that I wanted to contact my solicitor Mr. Winters. Whenever I gave the name he said something like, 'Mr. Winters would have plenty of dealings with those sort of people.'"
W	Castlereagh	22/6	"They didn't assault me at all after I had seen my solicitor. They made smart remarks then that they supposed my solicitor advised me to say nothing. They said that all he was interested in was getting his money and making money out of me."

X	Castlereagh	19/6	"However when I was being processed at the start of the detention, I was asked who my solicitors were and I said they were Madden & Finucane. One of the uniformed police officers said something like, 'You's all pick them...' They asked me what my solicitor said to me and one of them said something like, 'I suppose it was the usual crack, remain silent.'"
Y	Castlereagh	16/6	"They made derogatory remarks about Pat Finucane. One of the ordinary RUC men said something like, 'Sure that cunt's dead. Sure I'll go and dig him up.' Other policemen said, 'Isn't it a wonder all the provies get them.' He was referring to my choice of solicitor, Madden & Finucane. This was said at the very start and by uniformed policemen just when I had been taken into Castlereagh and was being processed.
Z	Castlereagh	29/7	"They were also abusive about my solicitor Kevin Winters. They said that he was a murderer and that they would stiff him."
AA	Castlereagh	29/7	"When I had seen my solicitor, the police asked me did my solicitor not tell me to talk to them. They said that my solicitor had briefed me well."
BB	Castlereagh	29/7	"After I had seen my solicitor on Friday, they said that my solicitor would sink me because he advised me to remain silent... They refer to my solicitor by his first name, Kevin."
CC	Castlereagh	/7/90	"I told them who my solicitor was and they said that they might have known it was Kevin Winters, one of them had a quiet laugh to himself. ...they mentioned my solicitor during interviews and refer to him as the Gallagher man. I think they are making fun because he gave me cigarettes."

188

DD	Castlereagh	17/7	"I should say that during the first interview they asked me who my solicitor was. They knew it was Kevin Winters. They said something like, 'Oh, you and him will go well together, he's a terrorist just like you. He'll tell you to keep quiet.'"
EE	Castlereagh	17/7	"At the second interview, they asked me who my solicitor was. One of them suggested Paddy McGrory another one said, 'Ah no, its Madden & Finucane minus Finucane...' After I had seen my solicitor, they talked about me being in Newcastle and Bundoran. This was just after I had spoke to my solicitor. I remember mentioning to my solicitor that my family were in Newcastle and Bundoran and that I had been there. I told my solicitor Kevin Winters this during the interview. I think it very funny that they all of a sudden mentioned this the first interview after I had seen my solicitor. ...they said that I got out. I think it was nearer towards the end. I remember one of the policemen asked me who was up to see me. He looked at the file and said something like, 'Ah, it was Kevin.'"
FF	Castlereagh	13/7	"At the interview, between 3:30 and 5:00 p.m., the detective asked had I seen my solicitor and I said yes. I told him that I would see him again later on that night and he said that I wouldn't, that this was not Butlins."
GG	Musgrave St.	29/7	"The duty sergeant asked me which firm he was out of and I said, 'Madden & Finucane.' The duty sergeant then said, 'Oh, you are one of those boys.' I didn't see my solicitor at all. They didn't phone him.
HH	Castlereagh	22/8	"Taken to cell and searched in cell. I asked why and they said, 'We have to search you after the solicitor's visits... One said the solicitor was young and the other one asked

who it was. He said, 'I don't know, I'll look it up after.'"

II	Castlereagh	20/8	"What did that bastard say to you, suppose they just told you to keep your mouth shut, they are only after the money. Madden & Finucane and Winters, they are just taking the blood money, the legal aid money is all blood money. They have made a fortune out of the troubles."
JJ	Castlereagh	2/10	"'Ah, who is your solicitor, Finucane?' He also said, 'We will see if we can arrange for you to meet him.'"
KK	Castlereagh	26/10	"The fat baldy one said that before Pat Finucane died he was in his house and he had a quiet drink with him. He said that your solicitor is going to tell you to keep calm and he is going to go back and tell the I.R.A. that everything is sound."
LL	Castlereagh	24/10	"They said that my solicitor was giving me very bad advice and that he was just a wanker."
MM	Castlereagh	22/10	"I just said that I wanted to see my solicitor, it's the only thing I've said. When I said this they just said something like, 'Madden and Madden and Madden and Madden etc.'"
NN	Castlereagh	2/10	"The ones yesterday were giving me a flak about the late Mr. Pat Finucane. They were saying that I must be well schooled saying nothing. They said that Finucane was well schooled just the same way and he got his just desserts. That was said earlier this morning by two detectives."
OO	Castlereagh	20/11	"They said that I was foolish to remain silent and my solicitor was giving bad advice. They said that he didn't give a fuck. They alleged that I am a member of the I.R.A. They said

that my solicitor was a dickhead and that he had sunk me and he was giving me bad advice."

PP	Castlereagh	8/11	"They started on about my solicitors. If I had seen my solicitor, they said that Pat was greedy for money. They said that I didn't know Pat Finucane had a close friend who is a detective inspector. The one who said this was a baldy ginger-haired fella. They referred to my solicitor just as Kevin Winters but they didn't say anything abusive about him."
QQ	Castlereagh	7/11	"They said that my solicitor mustn't think too much of me yet as he hadn't been in to see me."
RR	Castlereagh	8/11	"'I suppose your solicitor has advised you to say nothing.' ...They kept on going on about me remaining silent and asked me who my solicitors were. They referred to my solicitors as 'Mike and Bernie Winters, one up and coming problem.'"
SS	Castlereagh	5/11	"They said that my solicitor's advice was crap."
TT	Grosvenor Rd.	28/11	"Client and instructing solicitors were subjected to verbal abuse. Swenny made remarks about the firm, 'Yeah, Madden & Finucane are always causing us hassle, interfering so and sos. What are you using Madden & Finucane for? In the case of this nature, sure they make all their money from those provie types and all that criminal work.'"
UU	Castlereagh	31/12	"In relation to the solicitor they just said that the solicitor would just tell me to say nothing."
VV	Castlereagh	14/12	"We are deferring him for 24 hours, possibly 48 hours in case the solicitor gets in contact

191

with people outside. We know you are a wee chuck now because you have got Madden & Finucane in your case. It doesn't matter to Madden because he is just looking after the likes of Gerry Adams and Danny Morrisons of this world. They said, 'He likes to be seen with the big boys.' They said that remaining silent is only admitting your guilt. They then said that I was only a pay packet to Madden."

WW	Castlereagh	16/12	"They say that my solicitor was just a wanker and that if I talked I could cut my sentence in half. They said that I was getting bad advice. They said today that my solicitors Madden & Finucane were just rebel bastards and that they would get what Finucane got. This was said today before lunchtime Sunday 16/12/90. The abuse about the solicitor was the second interview last night, Saturday 15/12/90 between 7:00 p.m. and 9:00 p.m."
XX	Castlereagh	16/12	"They are going on about me remaining silent and about me being advised to remain silent and have been insistent on referring to deals and getting me to work for them."

1991

YY	Woodbourne	4/1/91	"They knew who my solicitor was. They said Kevin Winters and Pat Finucane were fireside solicitors. This was said to me on Sunday by the tall blonde-haired one. They said that the solicitor didn't give a fuck either because he was making £42 every time he comes up to see you. The tall one with the fair hair said this. They said that my solicitor would only tell me to remain silent anyway."

192